I0462178

Real World Colouring Book

For Advanced Users & Adults

Copyright 2019 By John Boom

50 Images

Created From Real Life Photos For You To Colour As You Please.

ISBN 978-0-359-82314-7
90000
9 780359 823147

CHAMPION

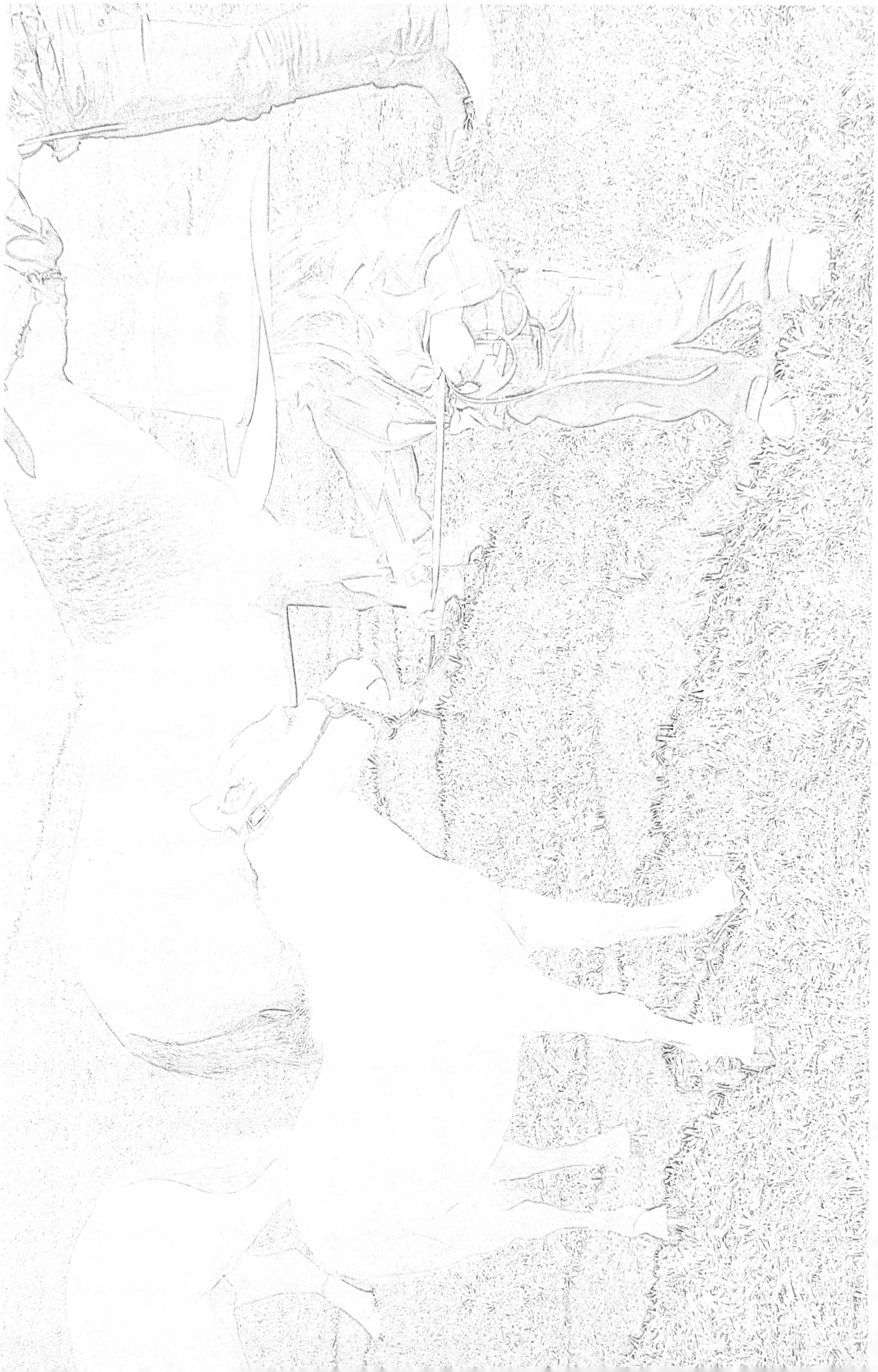

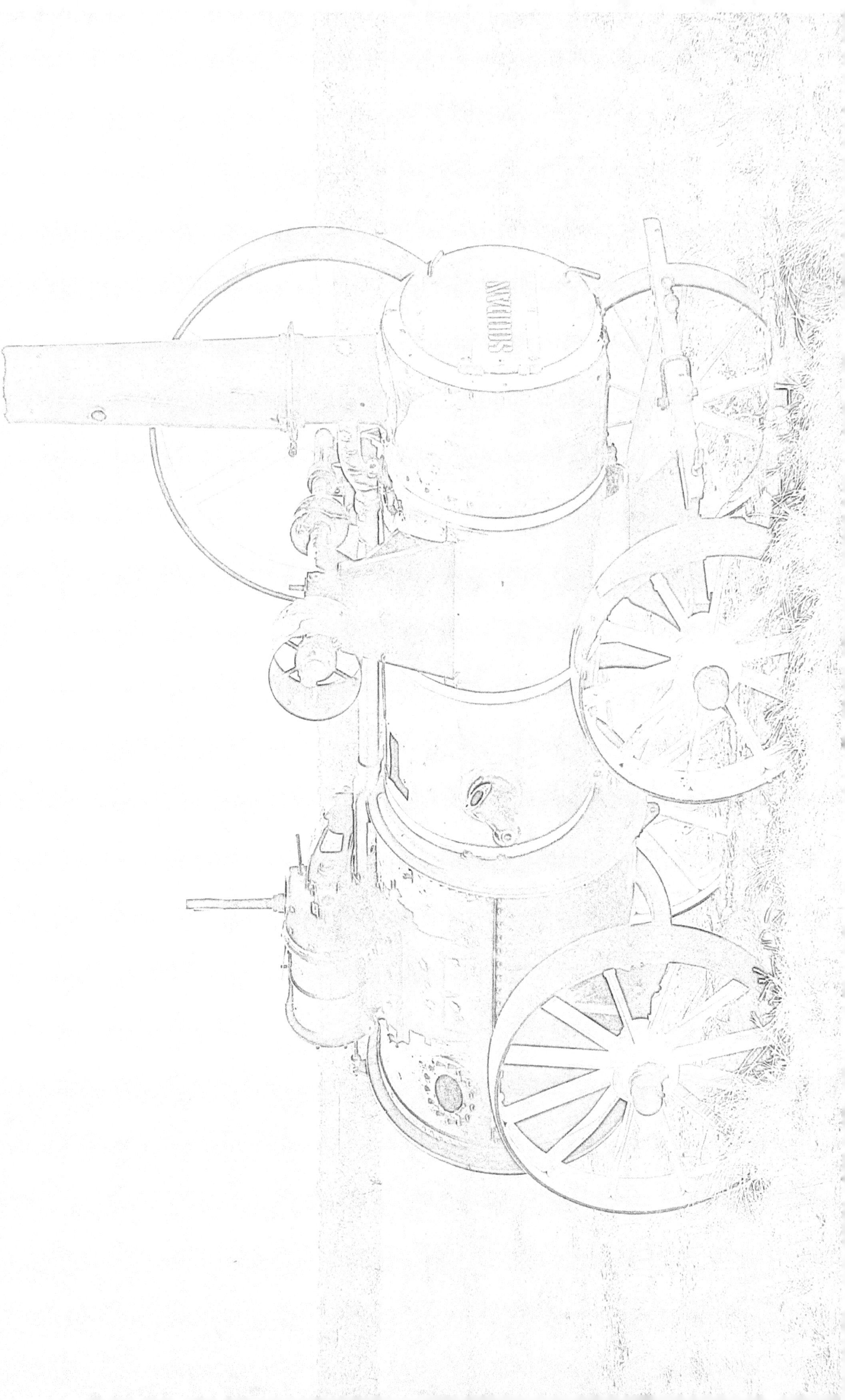

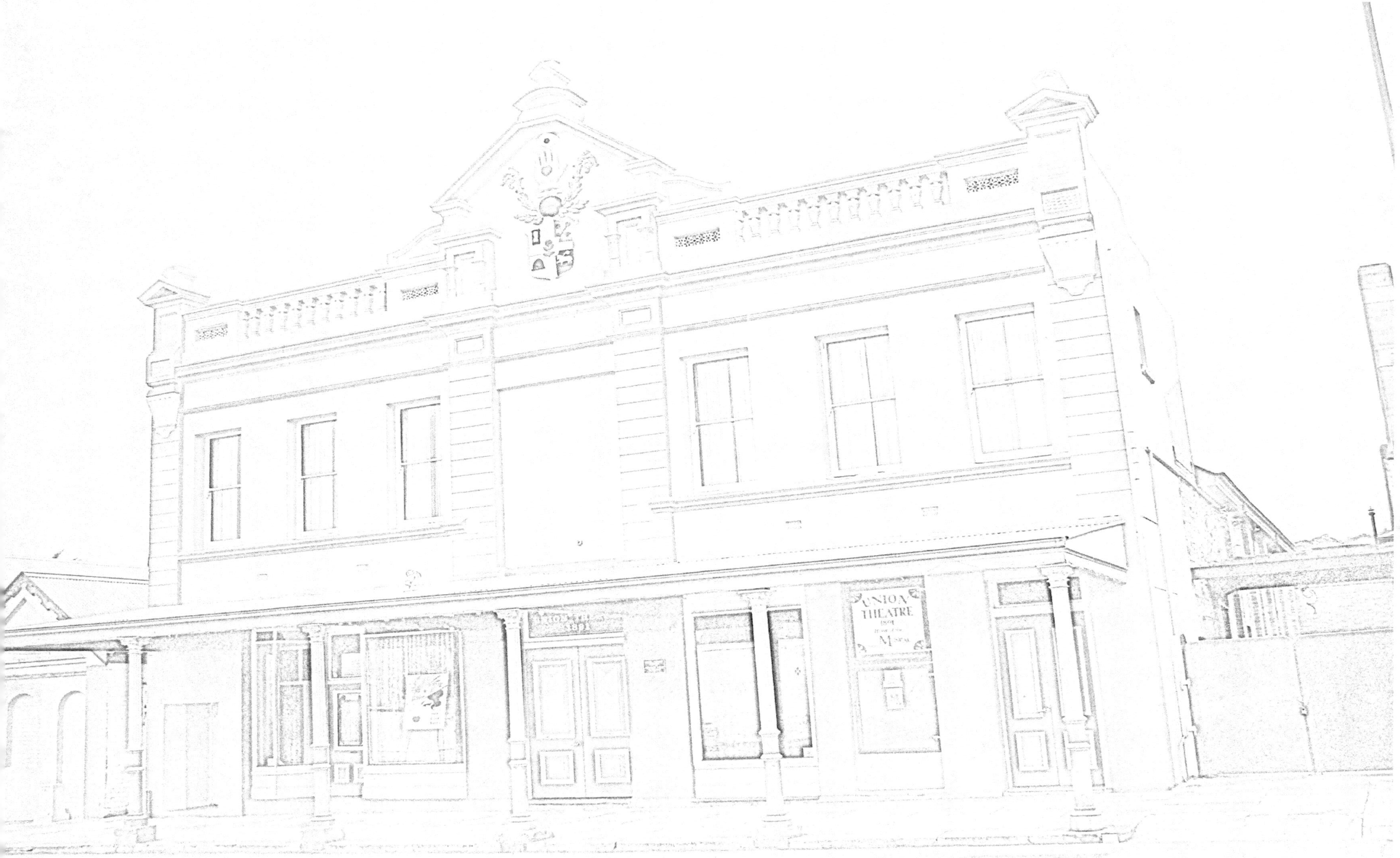
UNION
THEATRE

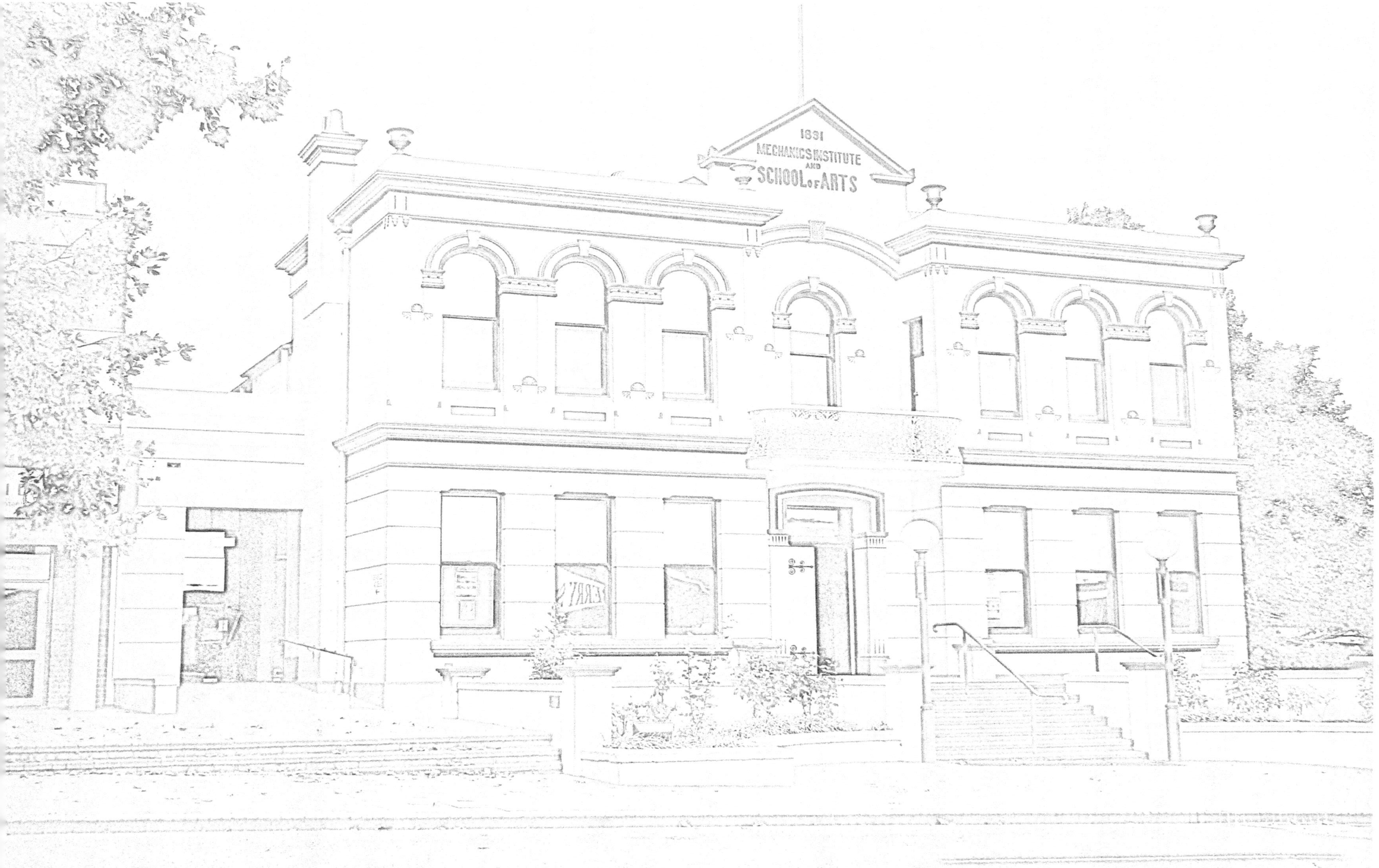
1831
MECHANICS INSTITUTE
AND
SCHOOL OF ARTS

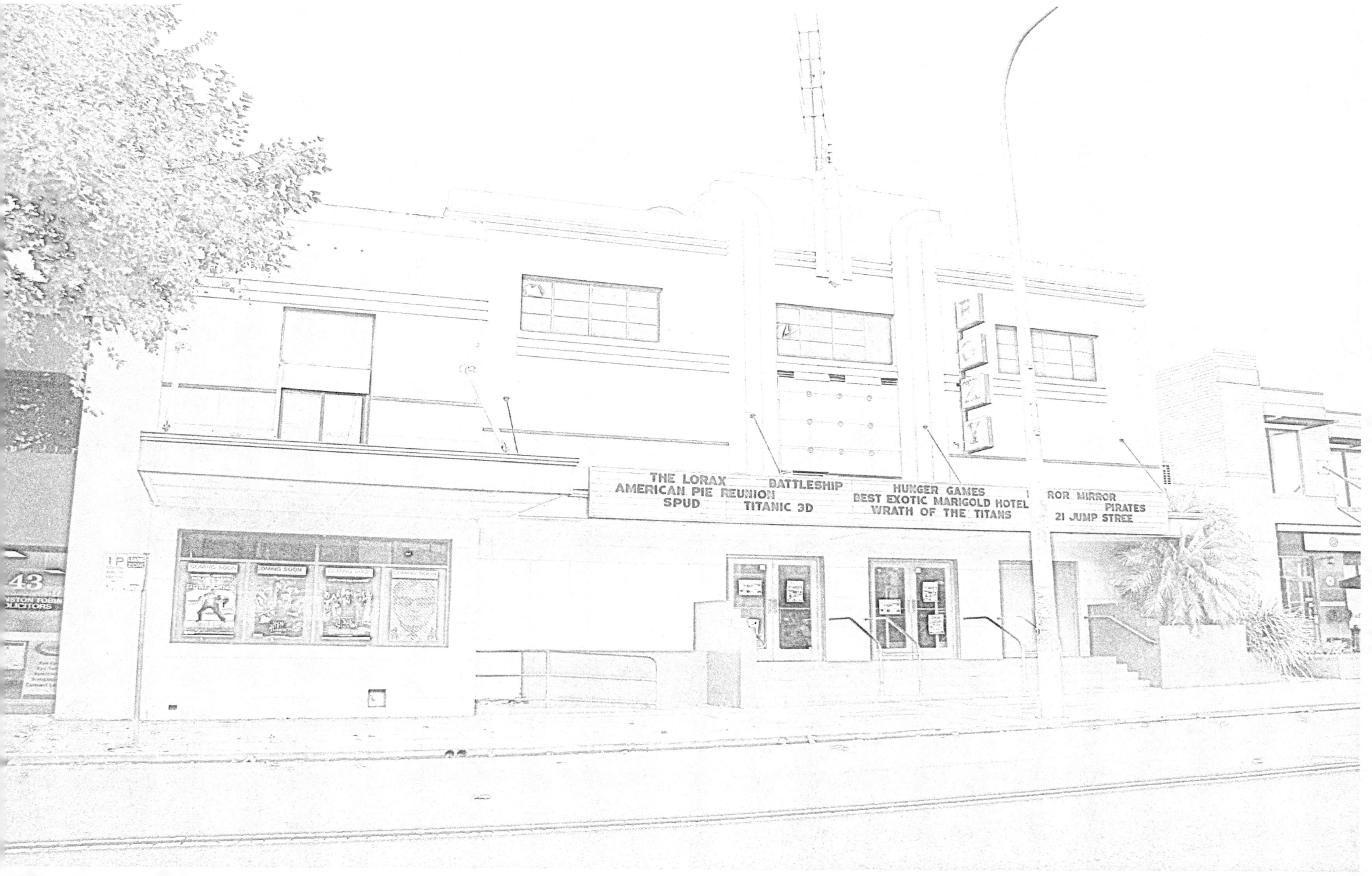
THE LORAX
AMERICAN PIE REUNION
SPUD
BATTLESHIP
TITANIC 3D
HUNGER GAMES
BEST EXOTIC MARIGOLD HOTEL
WRATH OF THE TITANS
ROR MIRROR
PIRATES
21 JUMP STREE
COMING SOON
COMING SOON
COMING SOON
1P
43

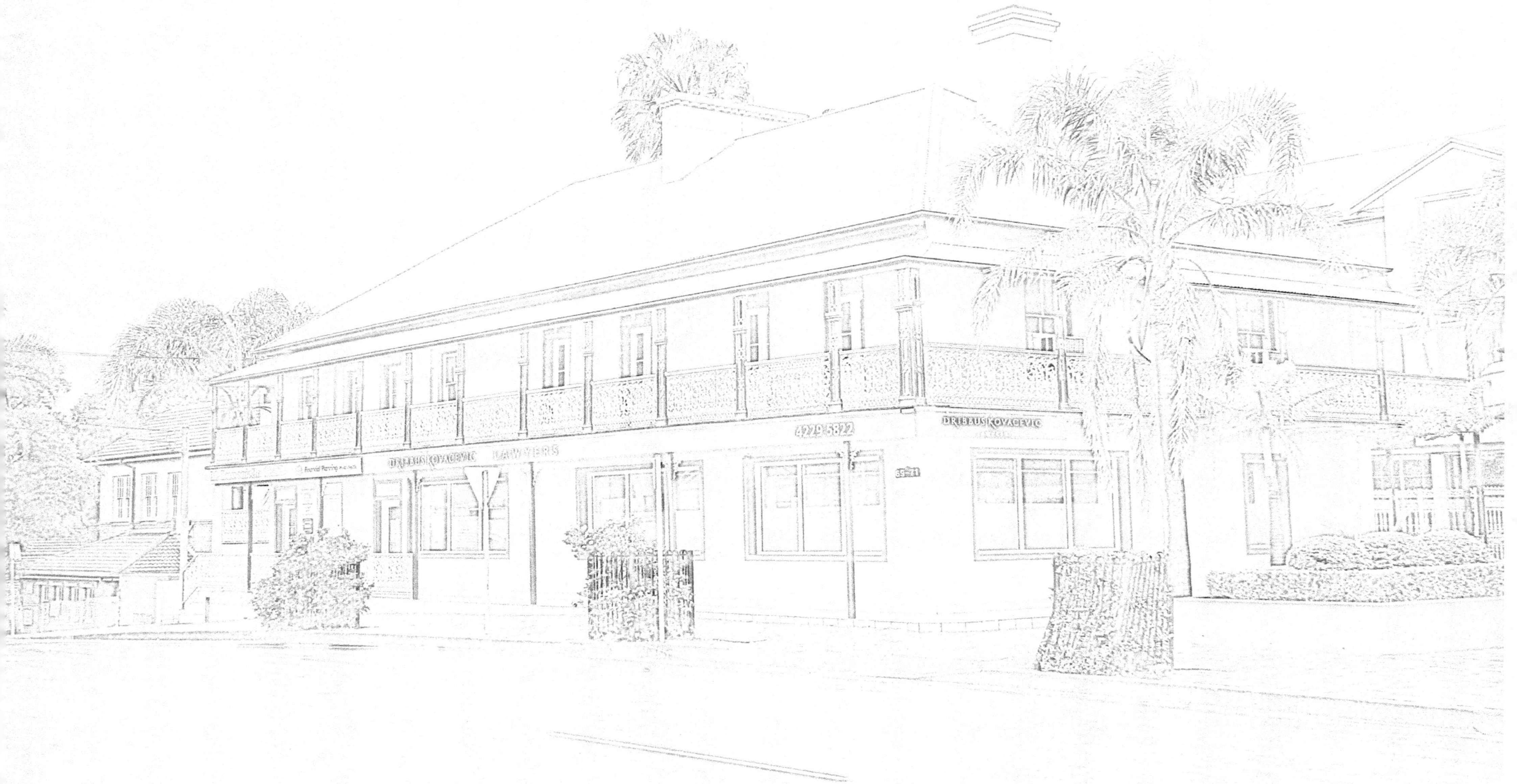

DRIBBUS KOVACEVIC
LAWYERS
4229 5822
69-71
DRIBBUS KOVACEVIC

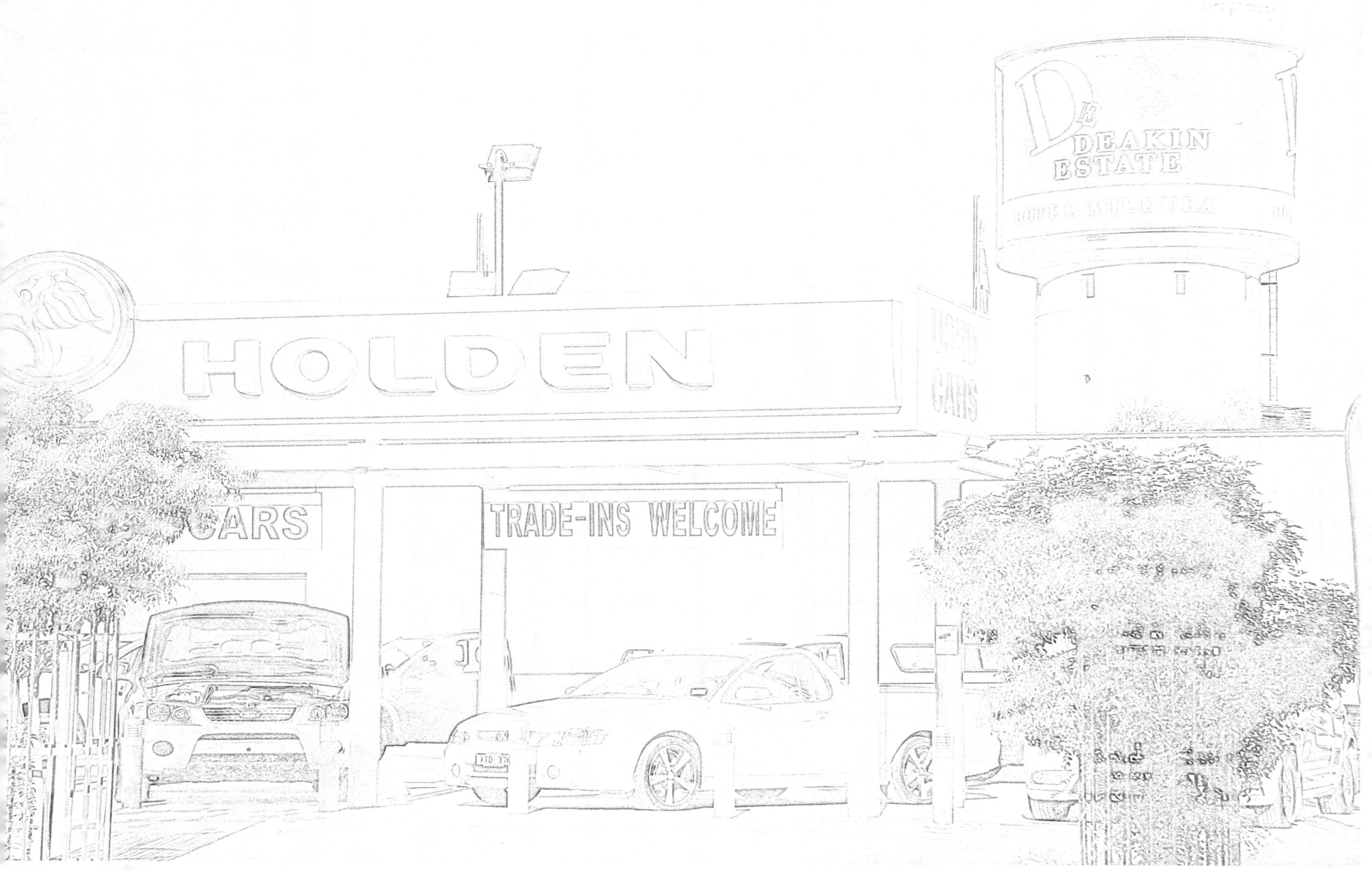
DEAKIN
ESTATE
HOLDEN
USED
CARS
CARS
TRADE-INS WELCOME

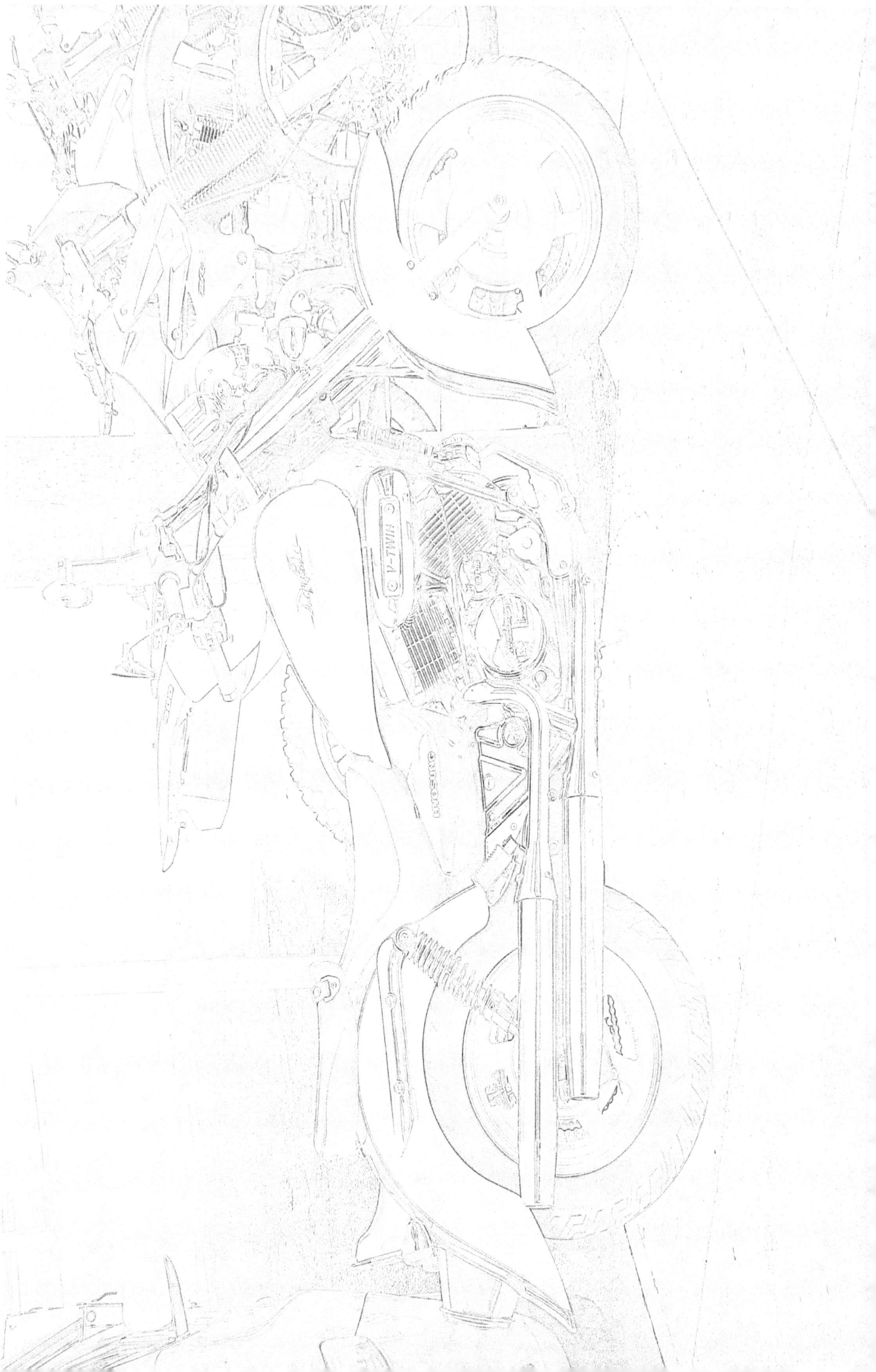

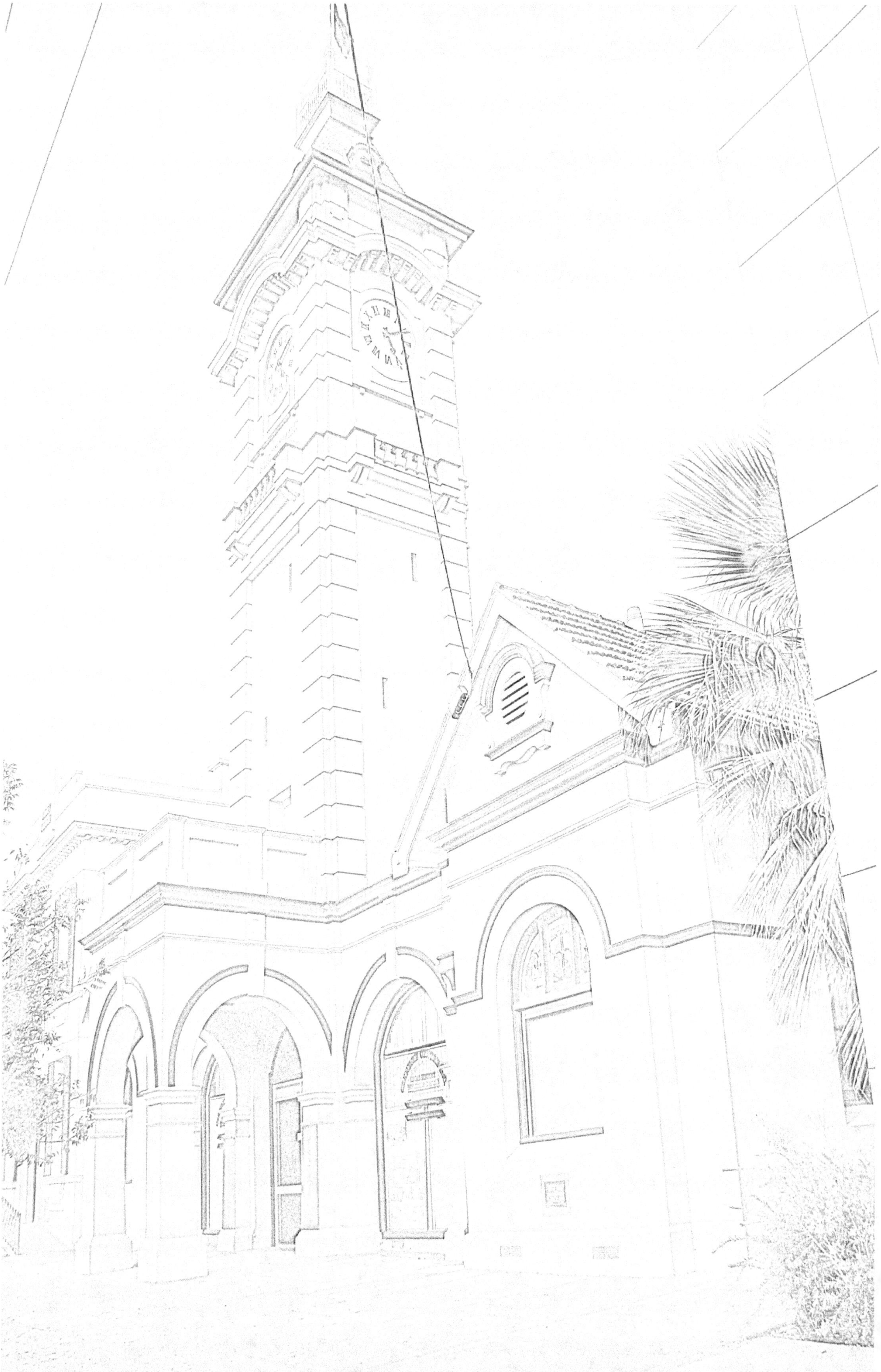

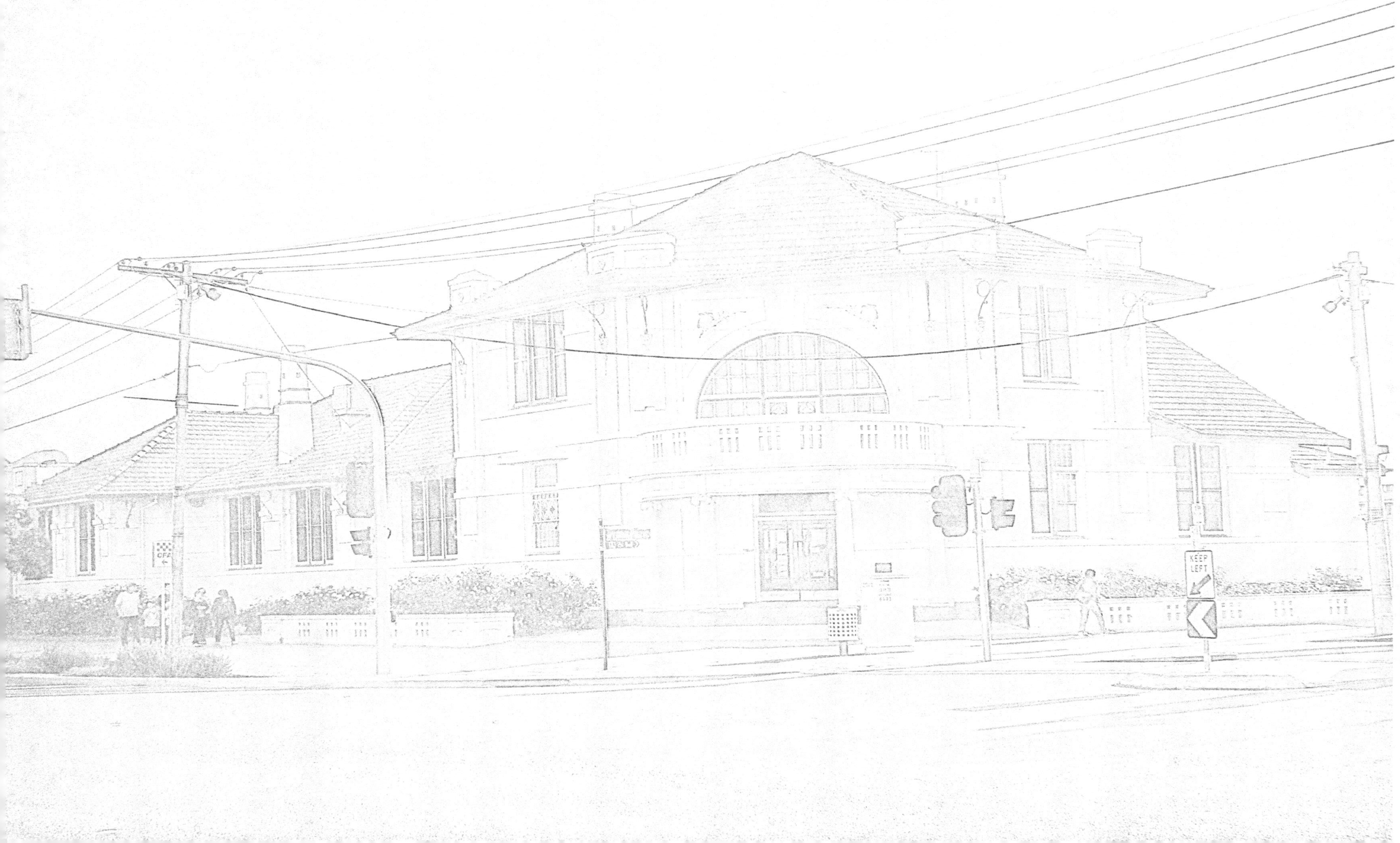
KEEP
LEFT

METHODIST CHURCH

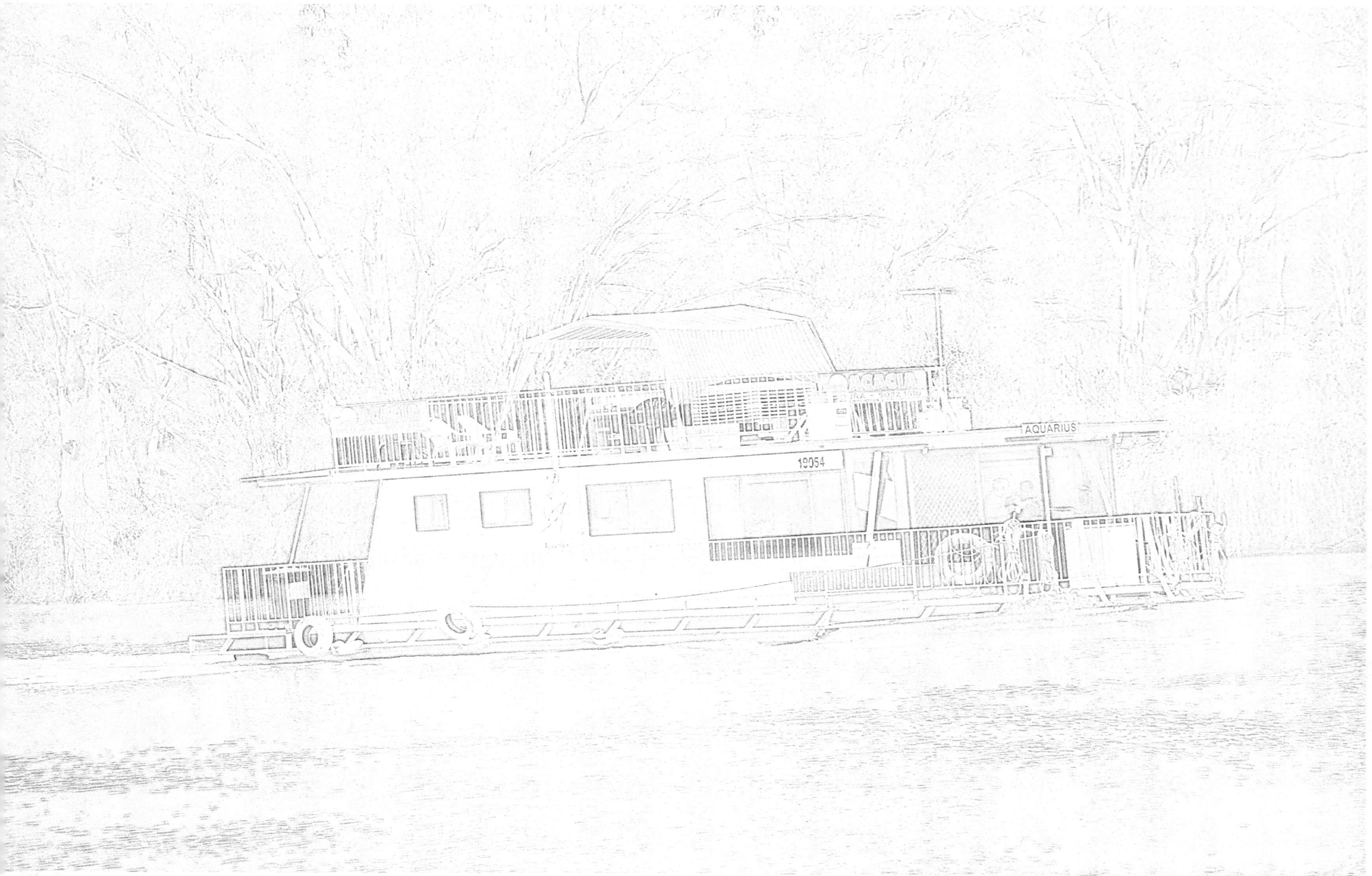
ACACIA
AQUARIUS
19054

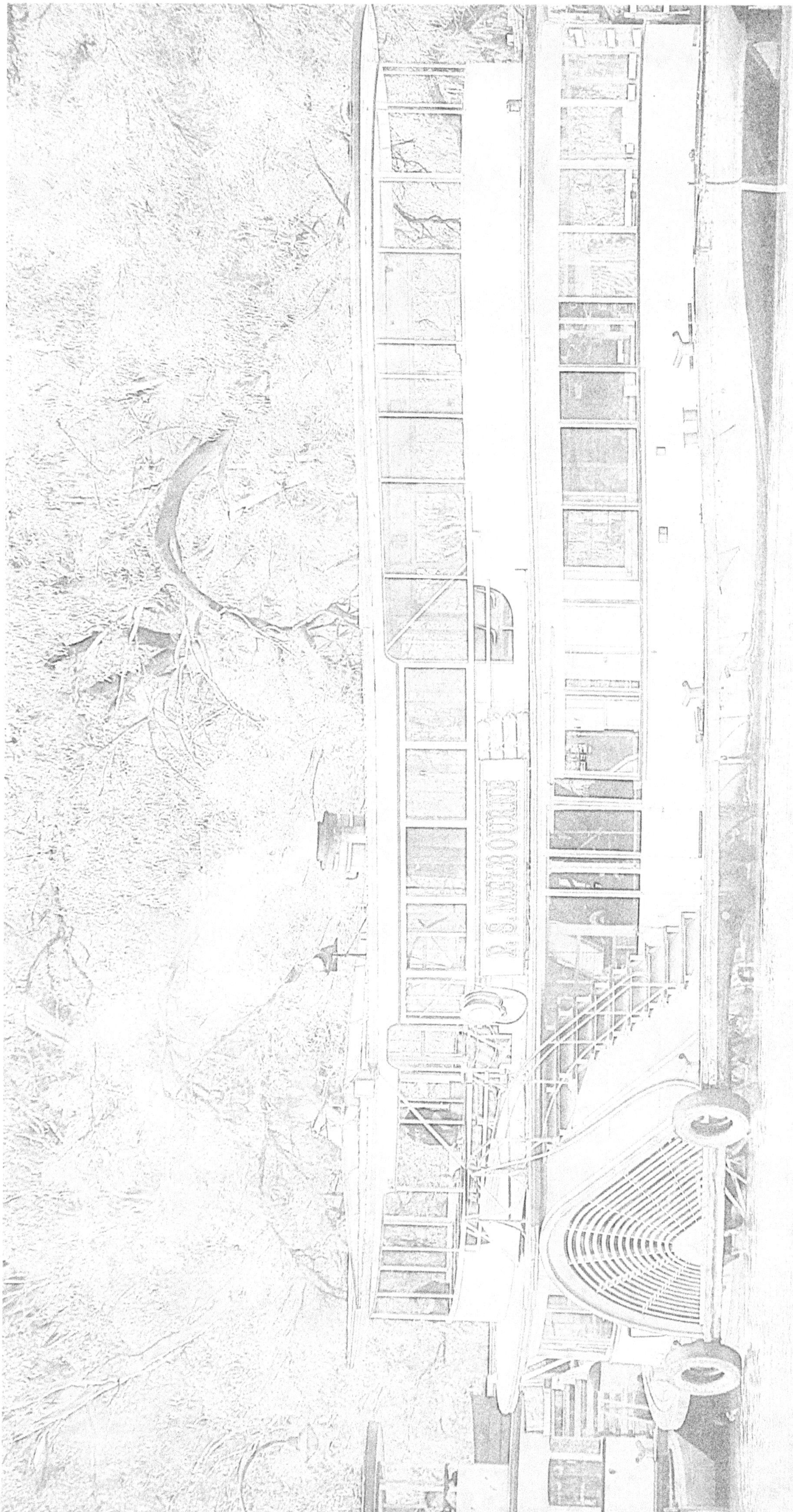
P.S. MELBOURNE

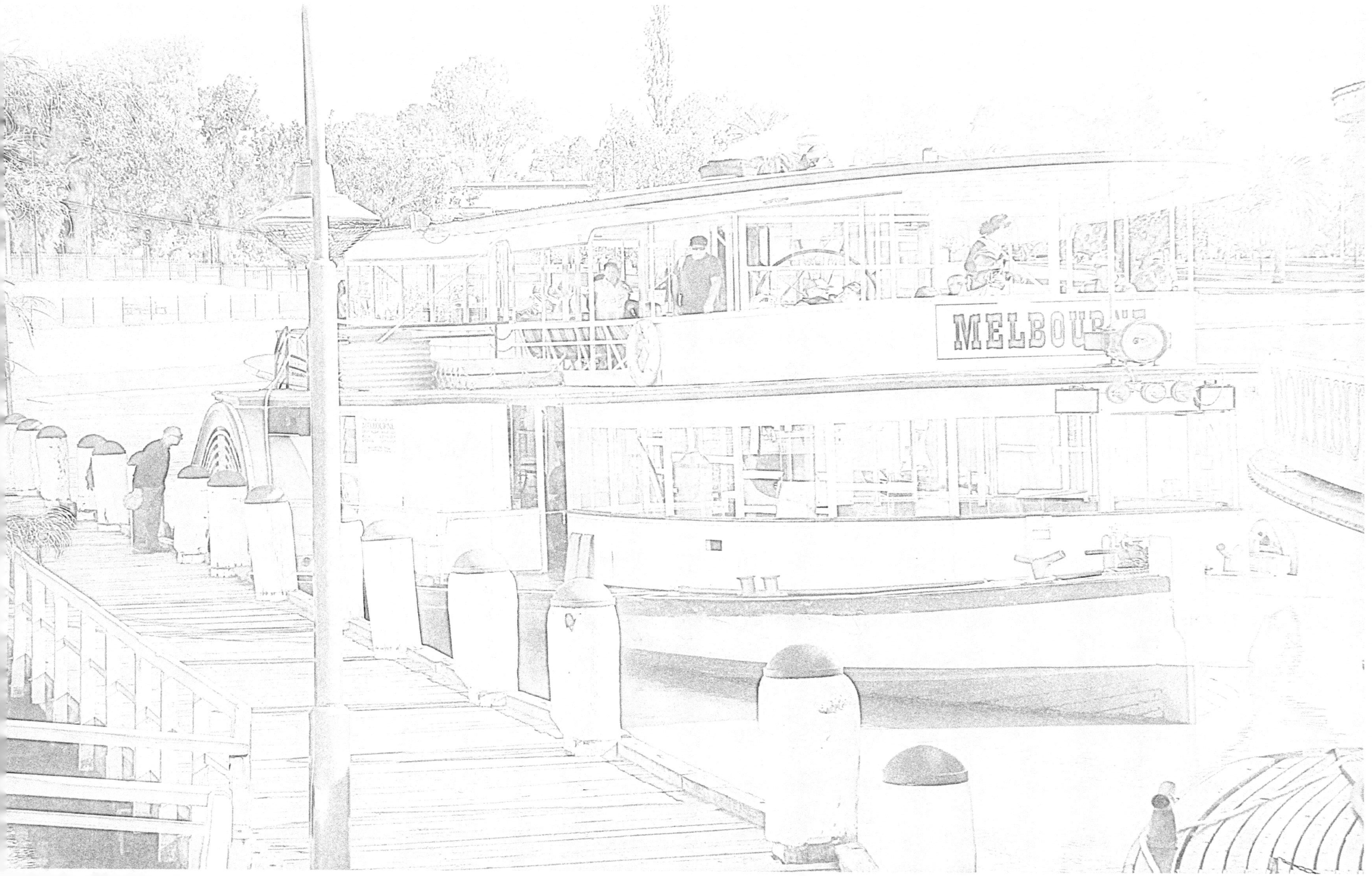
MELBOU

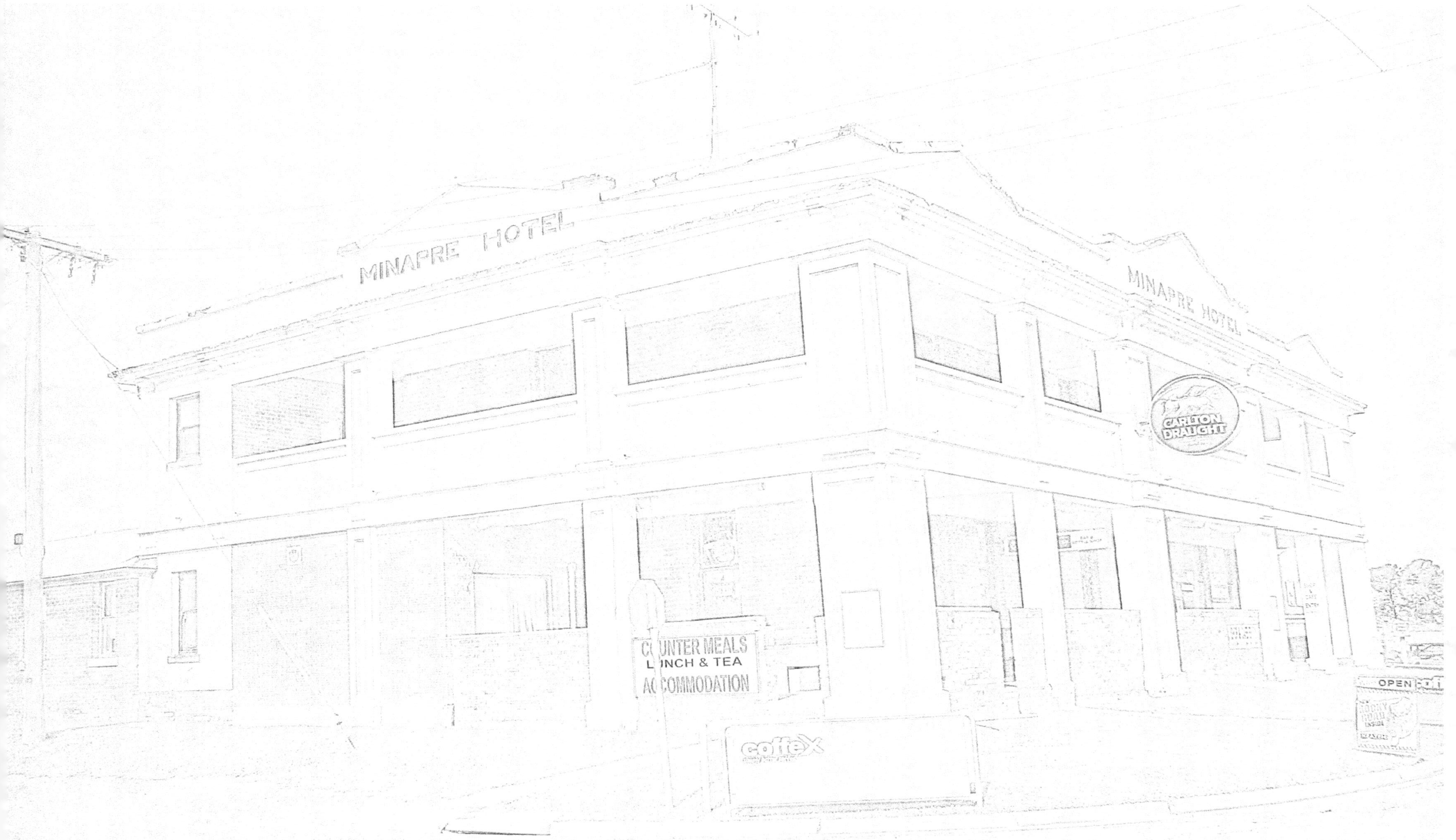
MINAPRE HOTEL
MINAPRE HOTEL
CARLTON DRAUGHT
COUNTER MEALS
LUNCH & TEA
ACCOMMODATION
coffex
OPEN

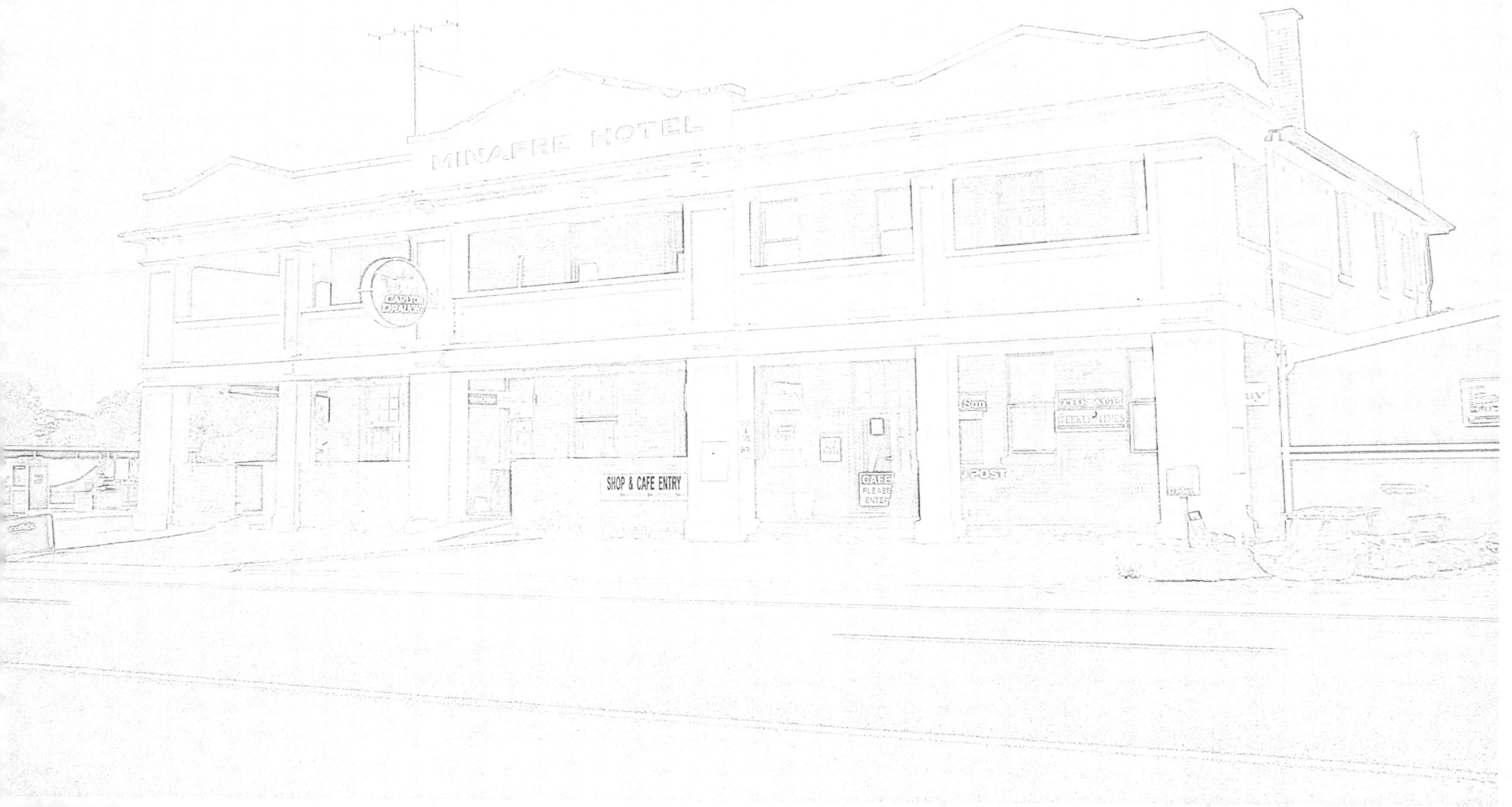
MINAFFIE HOTEL
CARLTON DRAUGHT
SHOP & CAFE ENTRY
CAFE PLEASE ENTER
POST
Sun
WEEKLY TIMES

The Nearly Outback Store
ANGLE PARKING
COFFEE SHOP OPEN

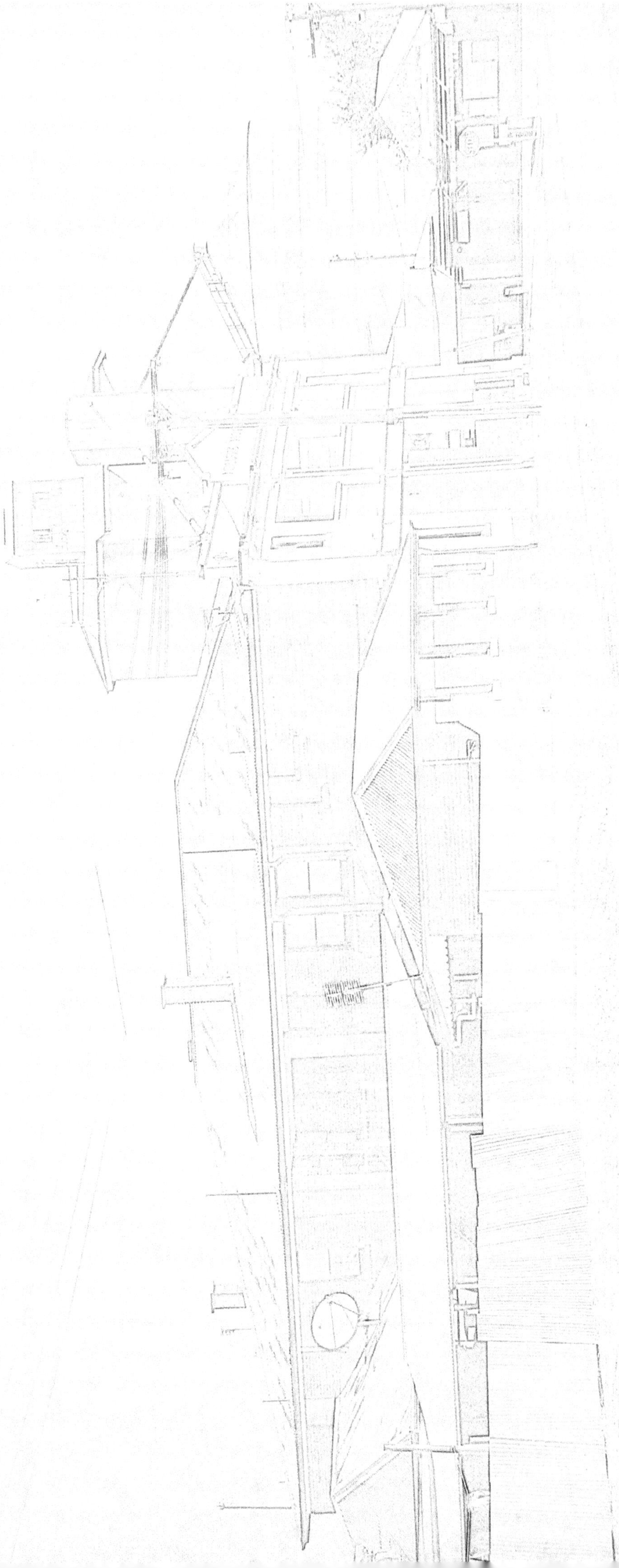

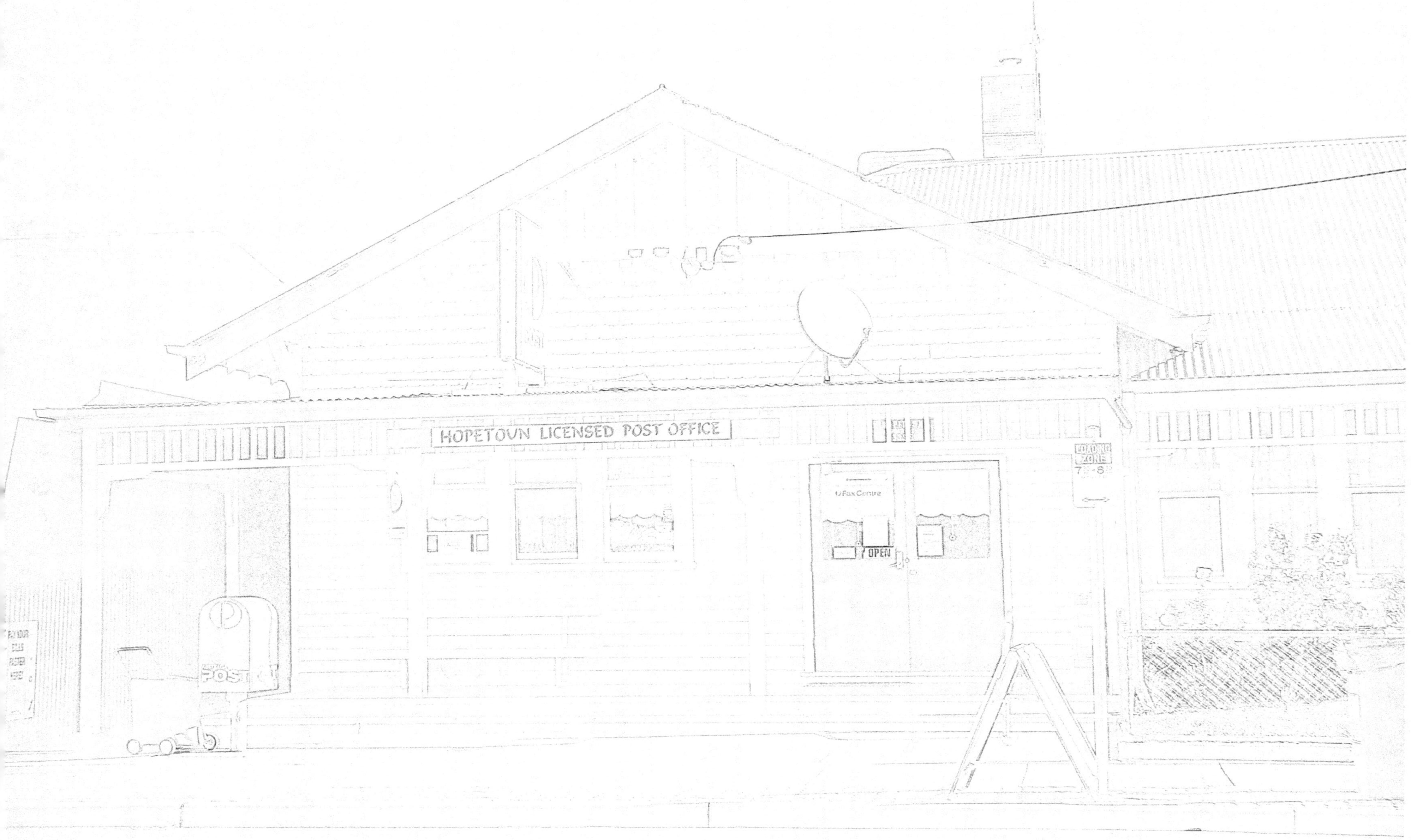
HOPETOWN LICENSED POST OFFICE
LOADING ZONE
FaxCentre
OPEN
POST

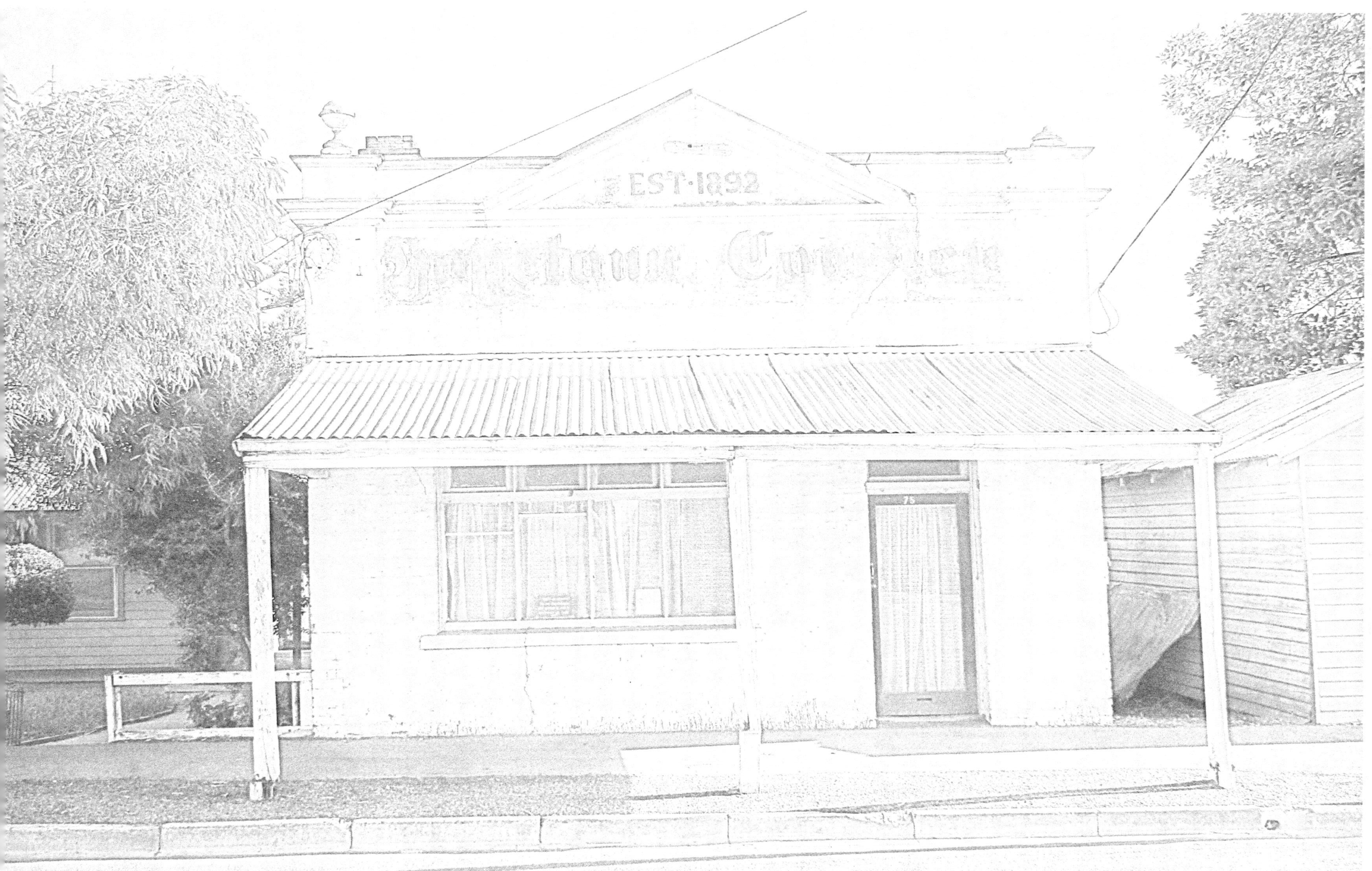
EST·1892

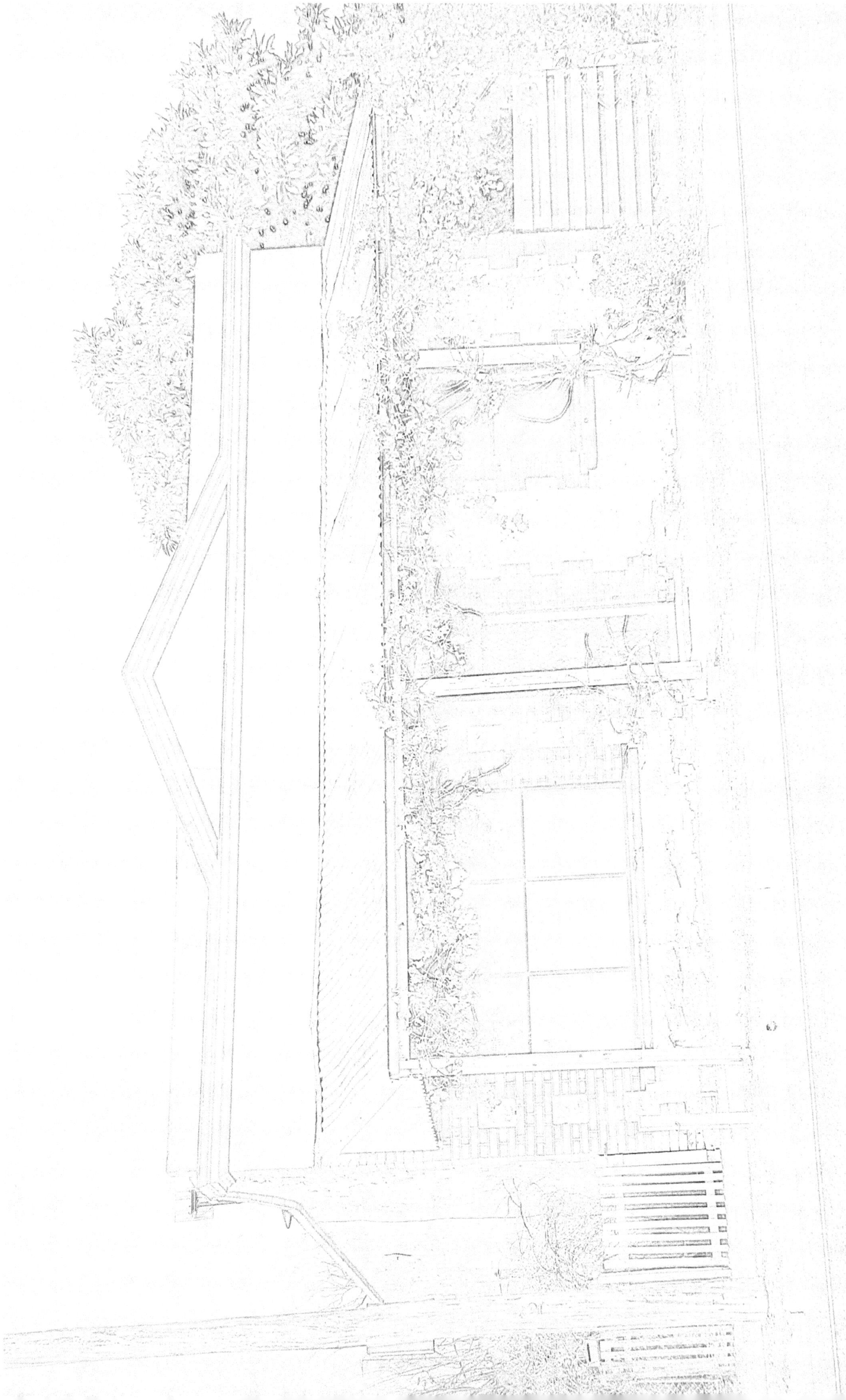

PRINTING
STATIONERY

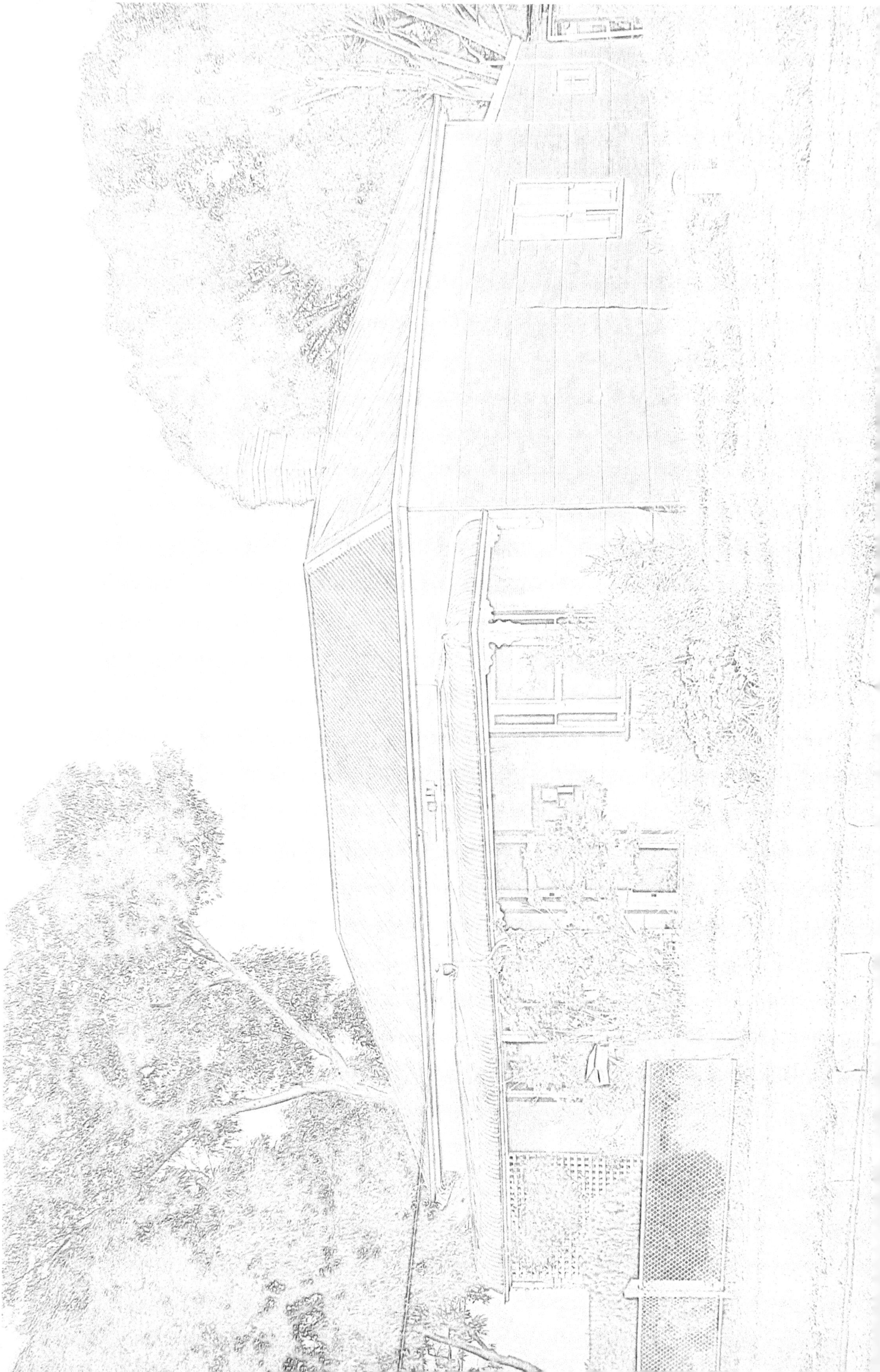

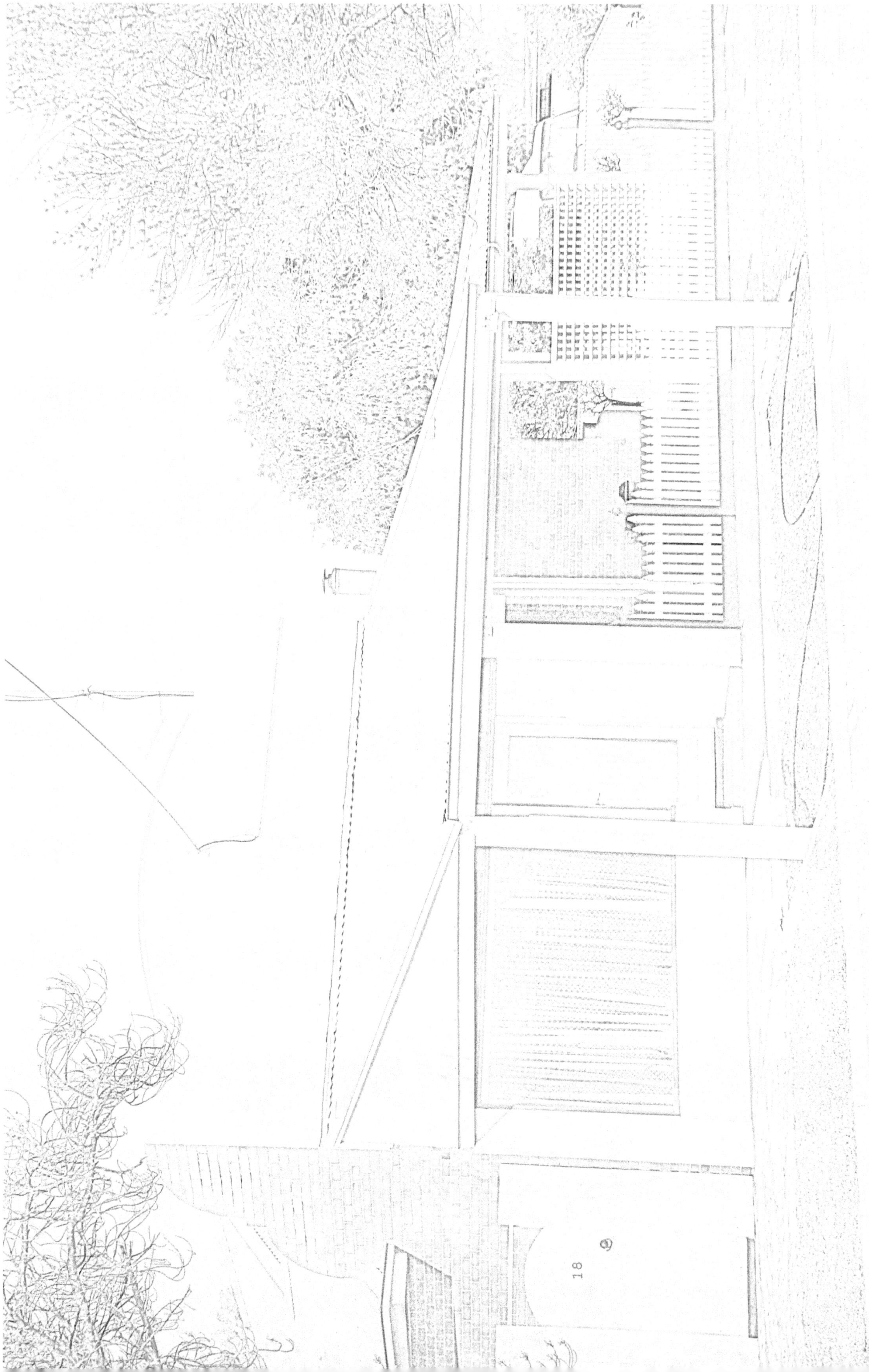
18

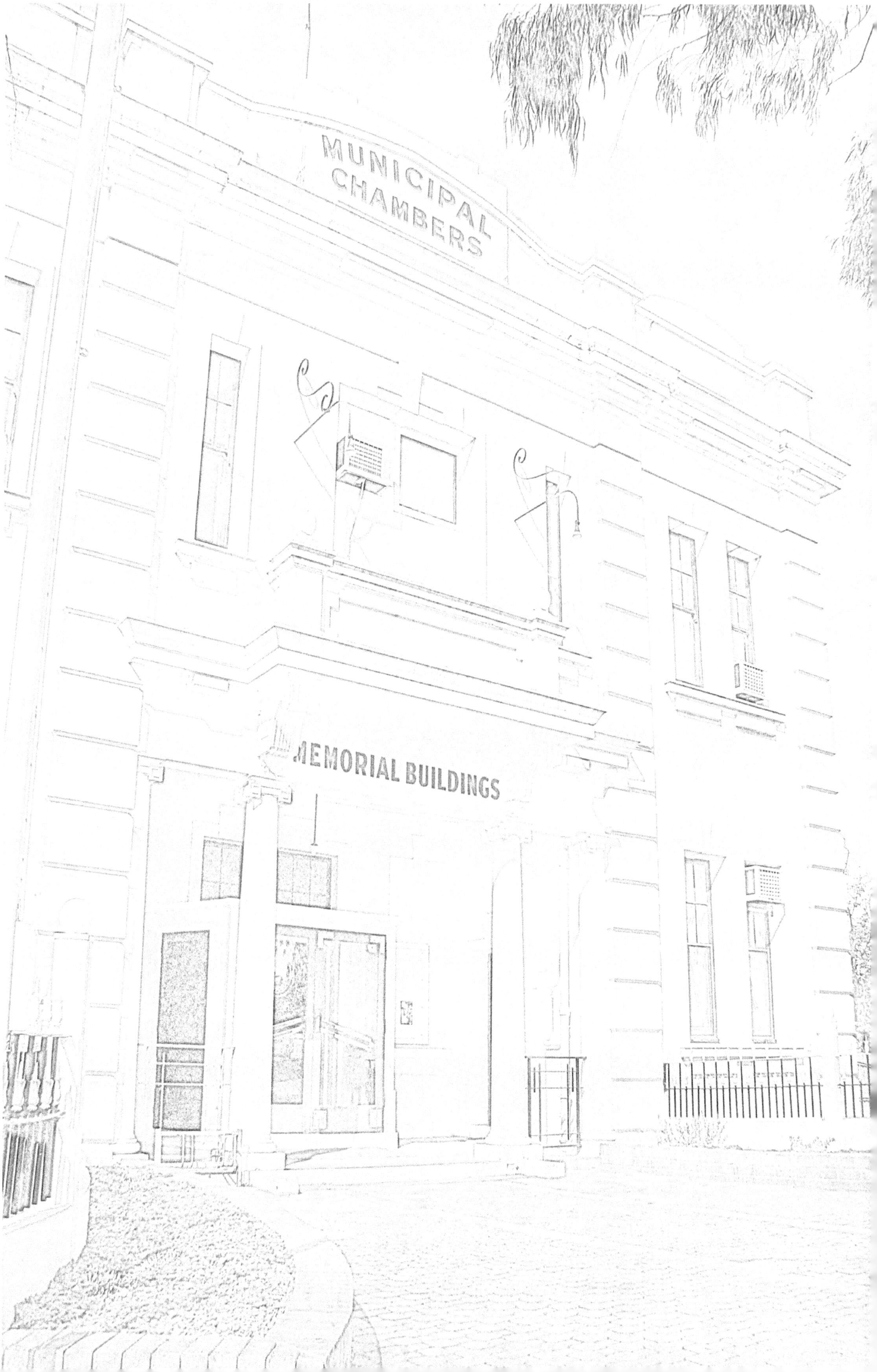
MUNICIPAL CHAMBERS
MEMORIAL BUILDINGS

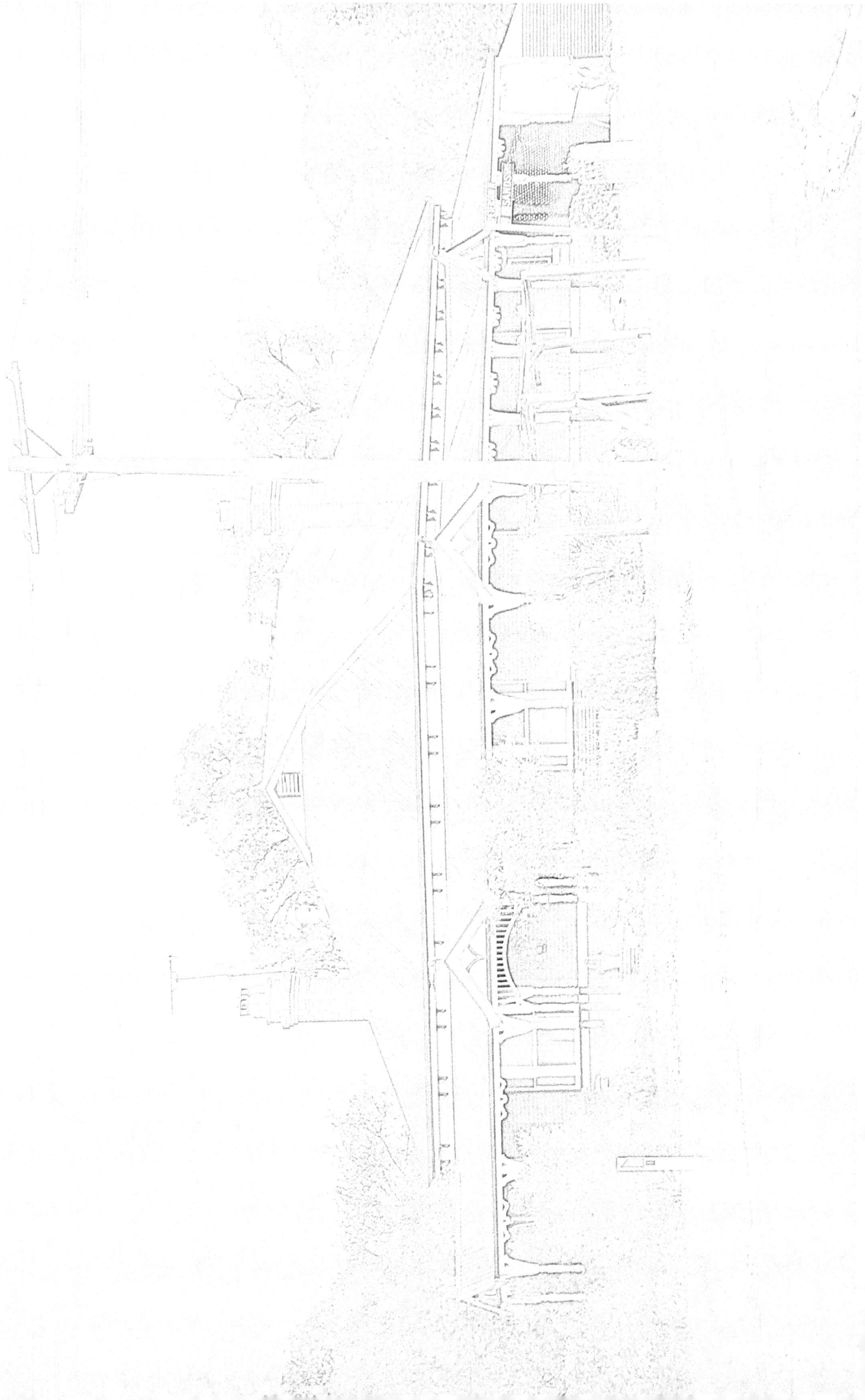

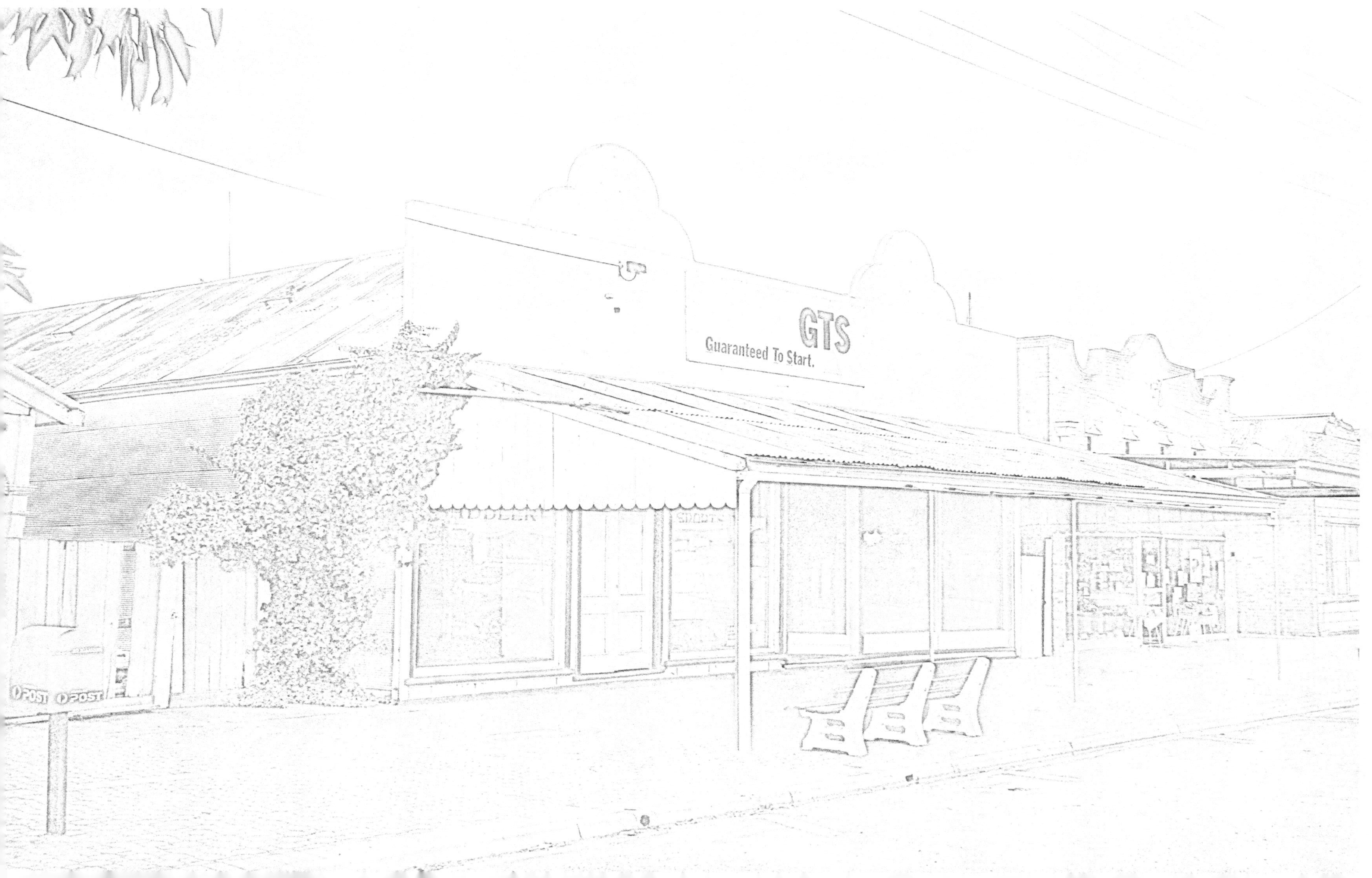
GTS
Guaranteed To Start.
POST
POST

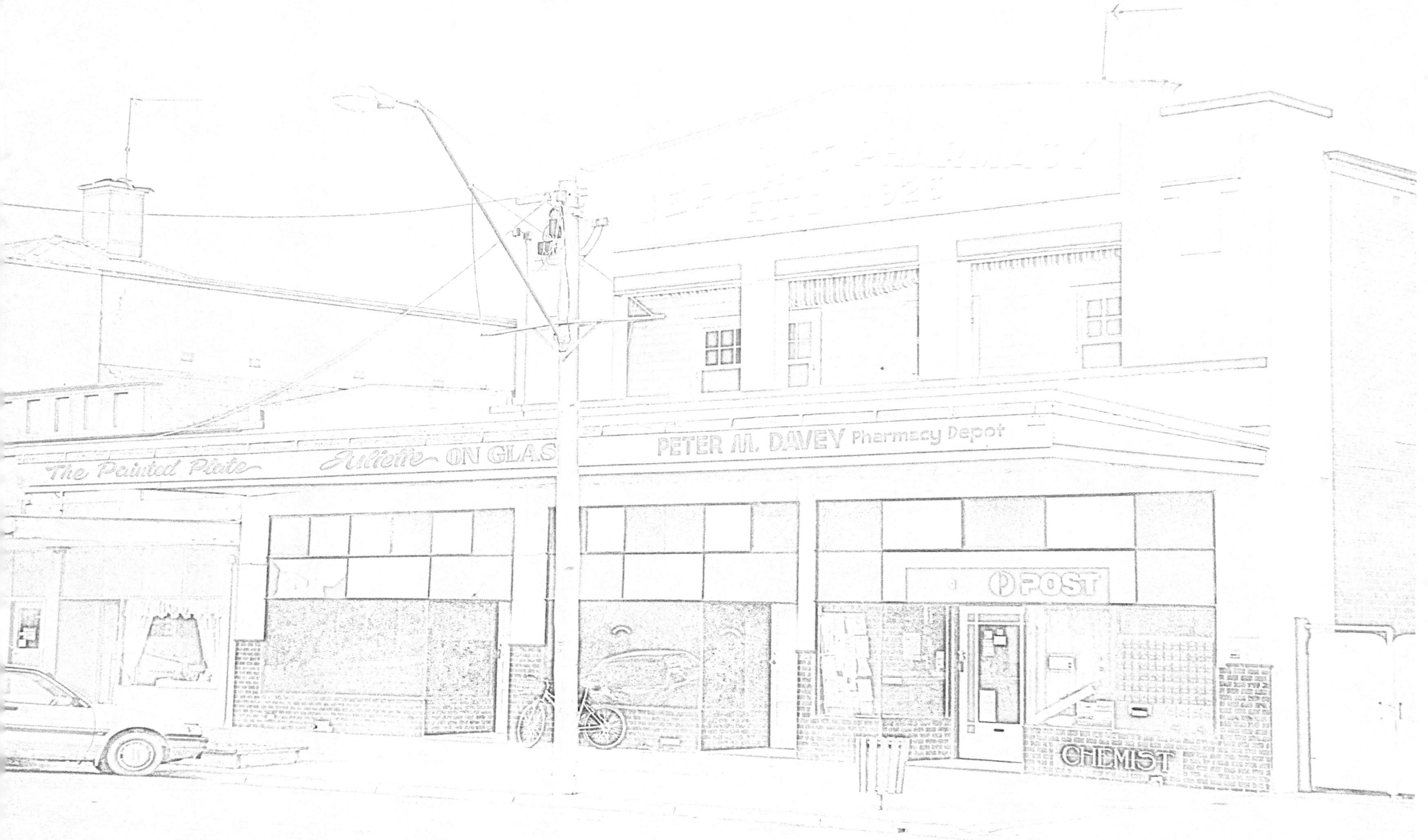
The Painted Plate
Juliette ON GLAS
PETER M. DAVEY Pharmacy Depot
POST
CHEMIST

POST

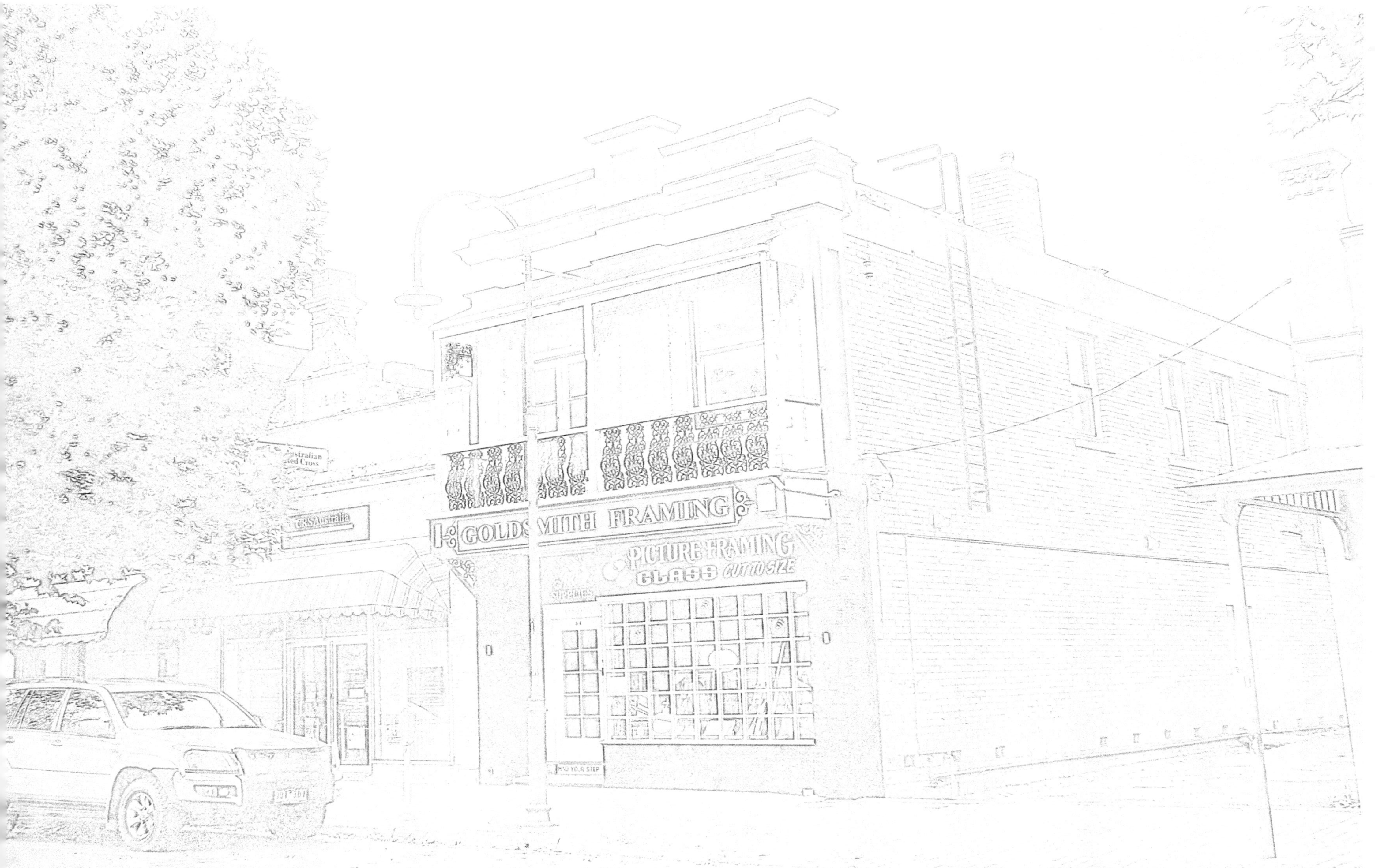
GOLDSMITH FRAMING
PICTURE FRAMING
GLASS CUT TO SIZE
SUPPLIES
MIND YOUR STEP
CRS Australia

HINDMARSH
SCOUNT LIQUOR

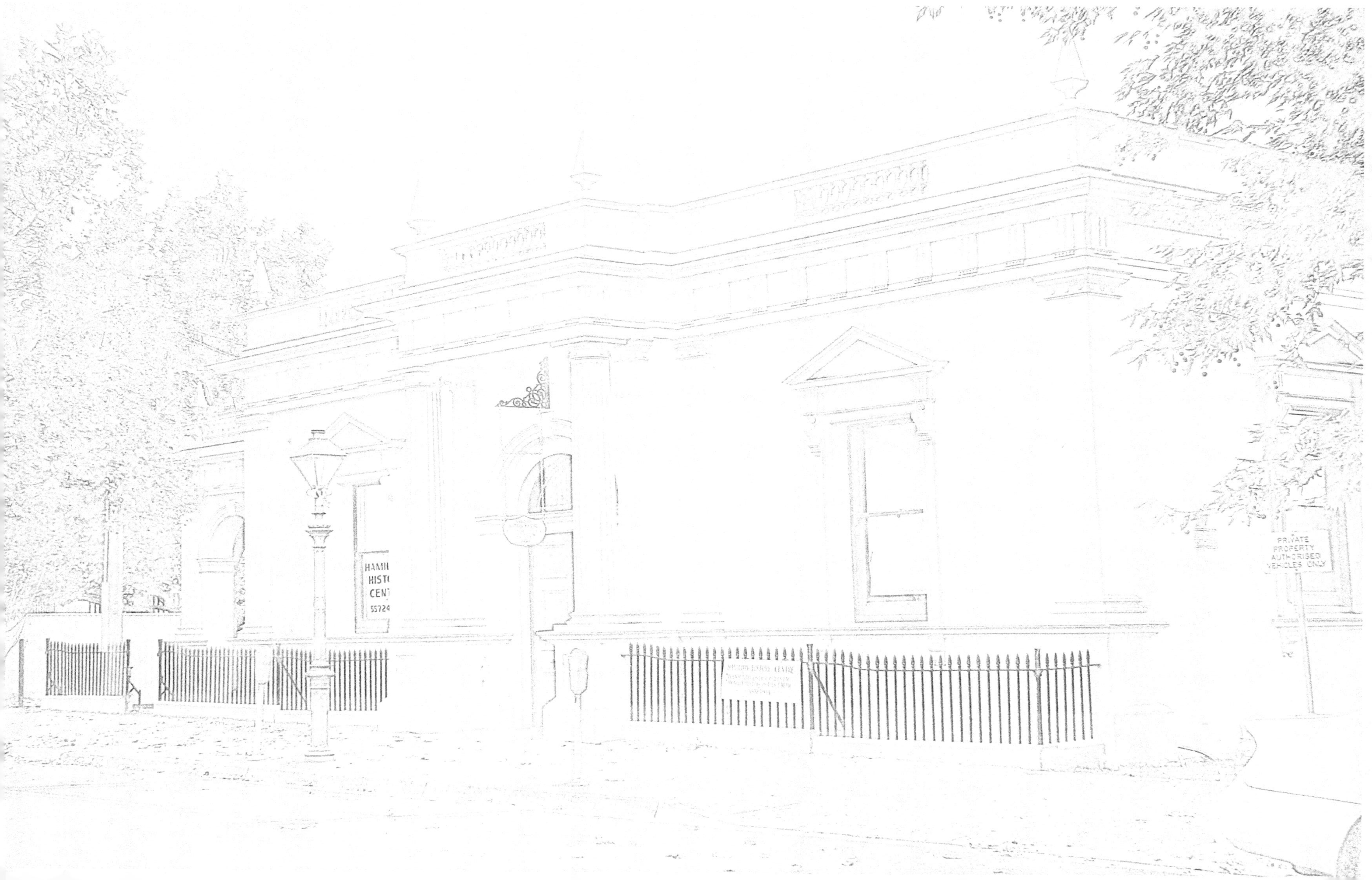
HAMI
HISTO
CENT
55724
PRIVATE
PROPERTY
AUTHORISED
VEHICLES ONLY

JEPARIT POST OFFICE

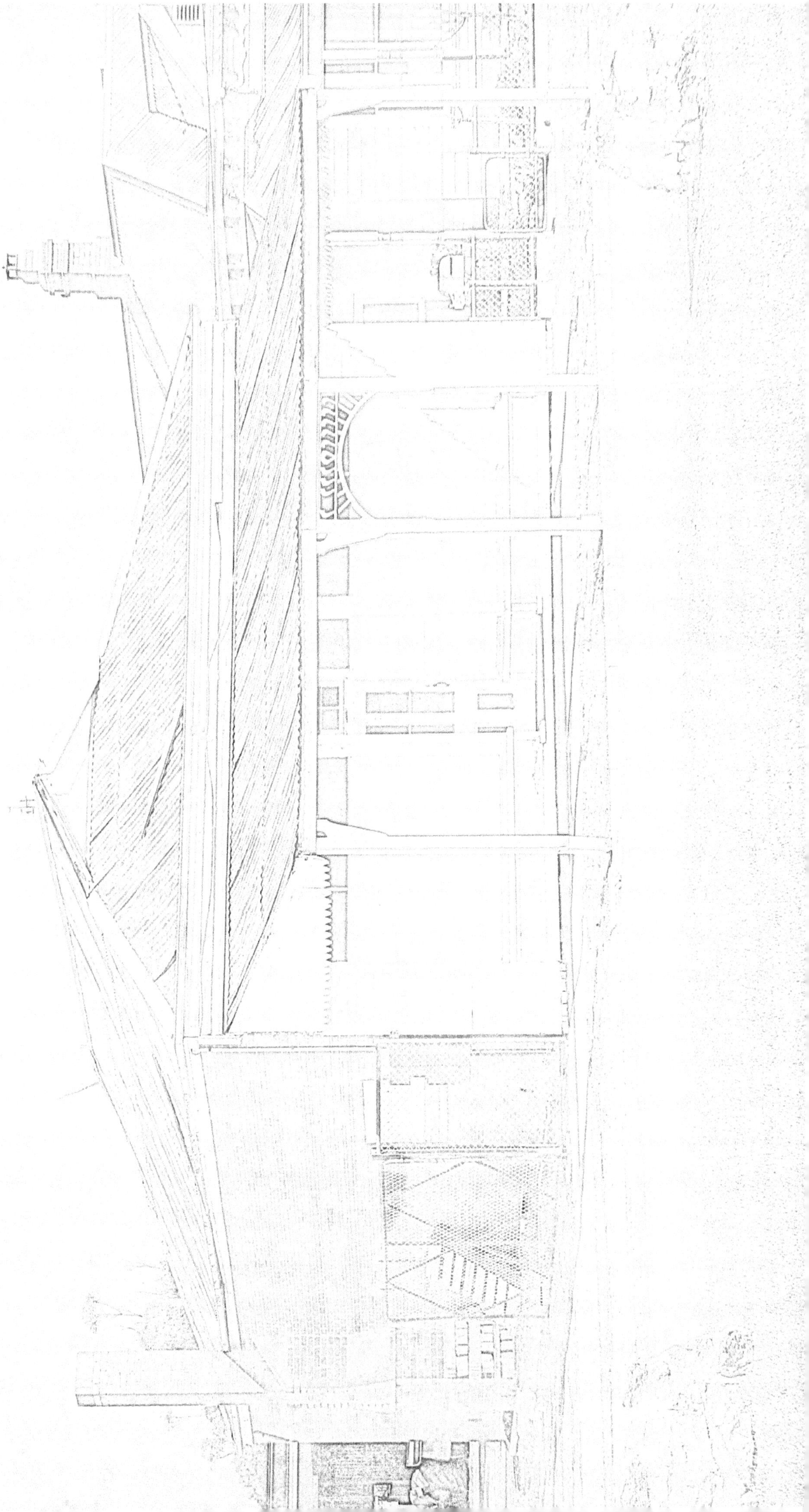

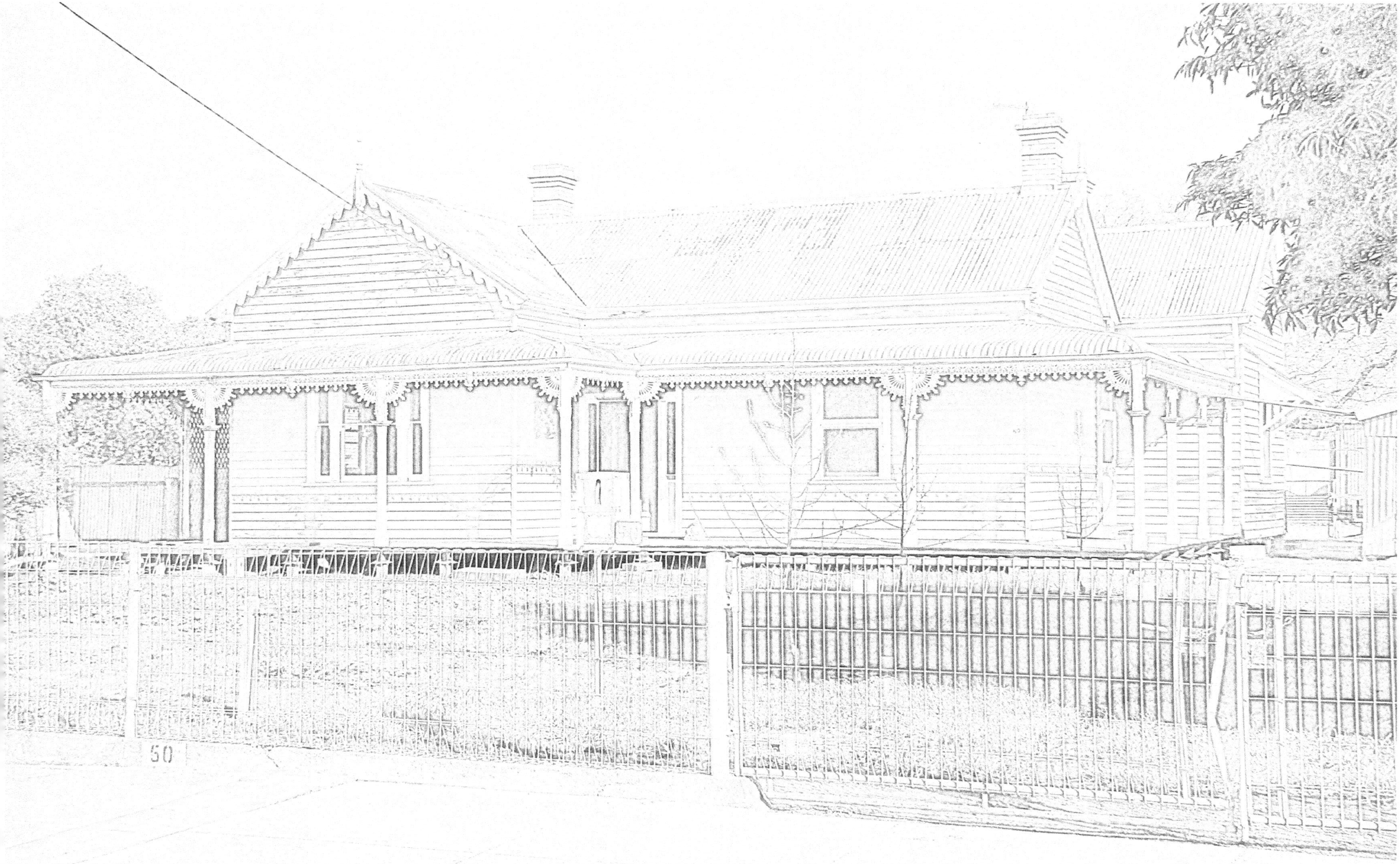
50

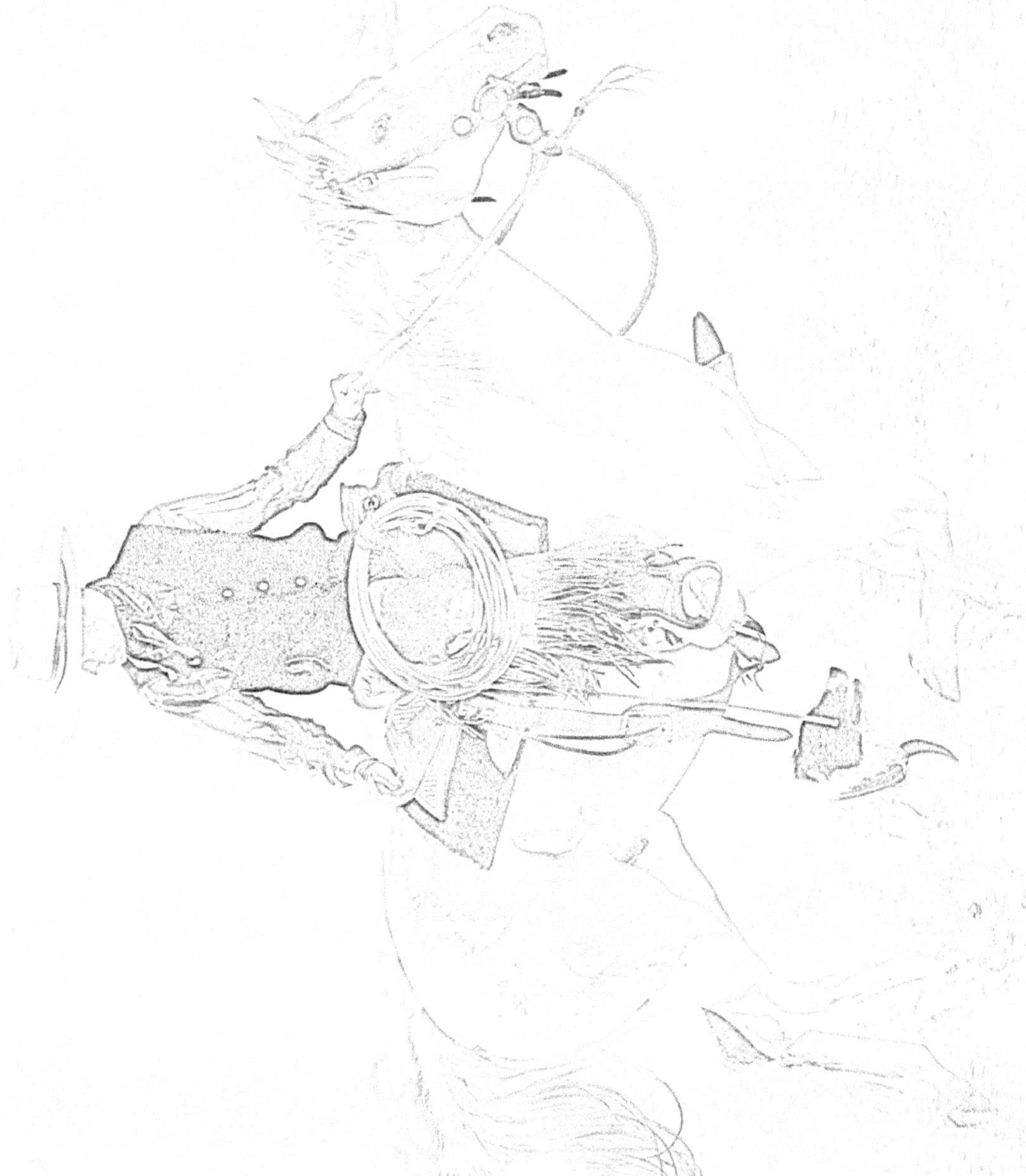

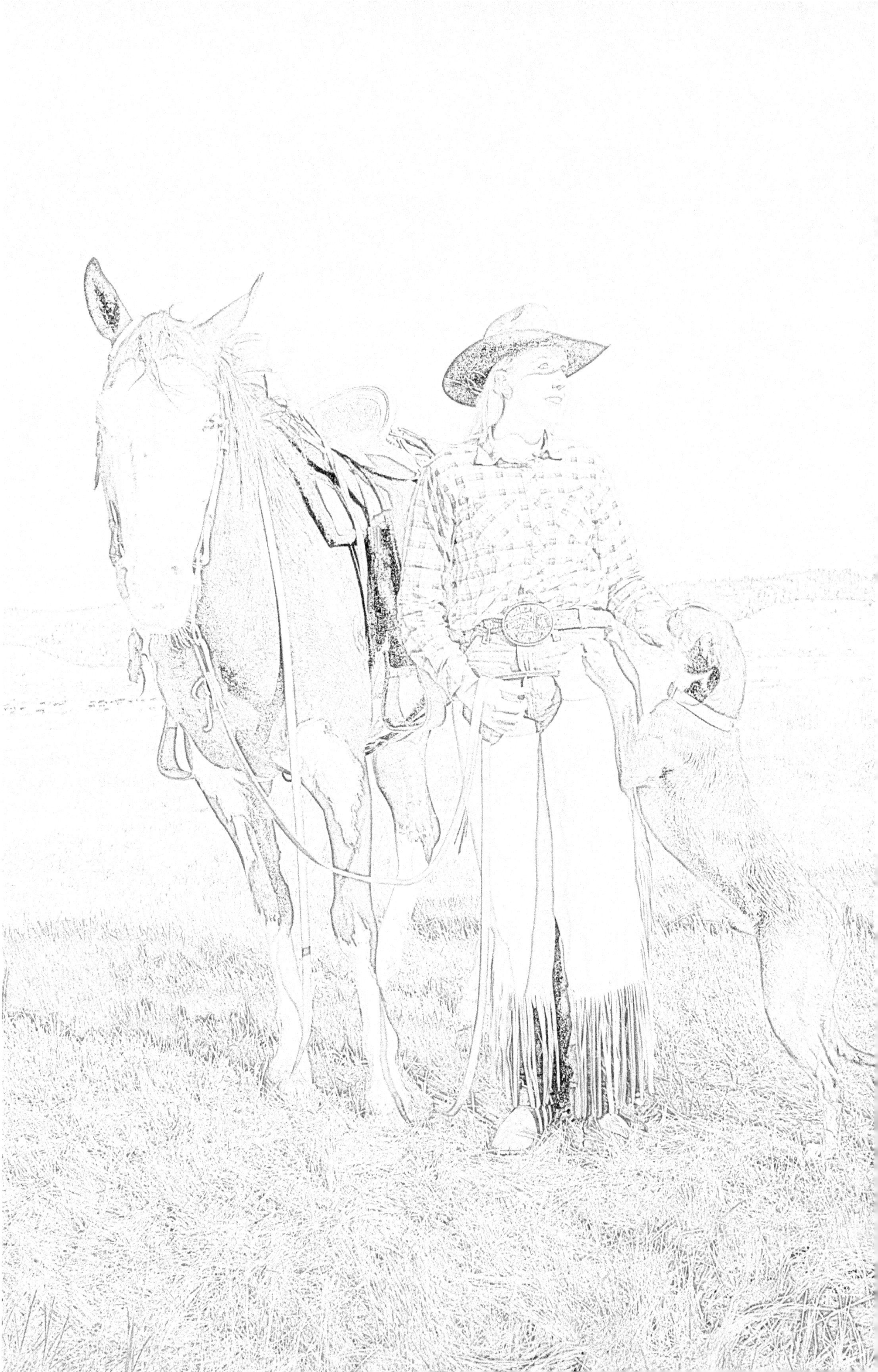

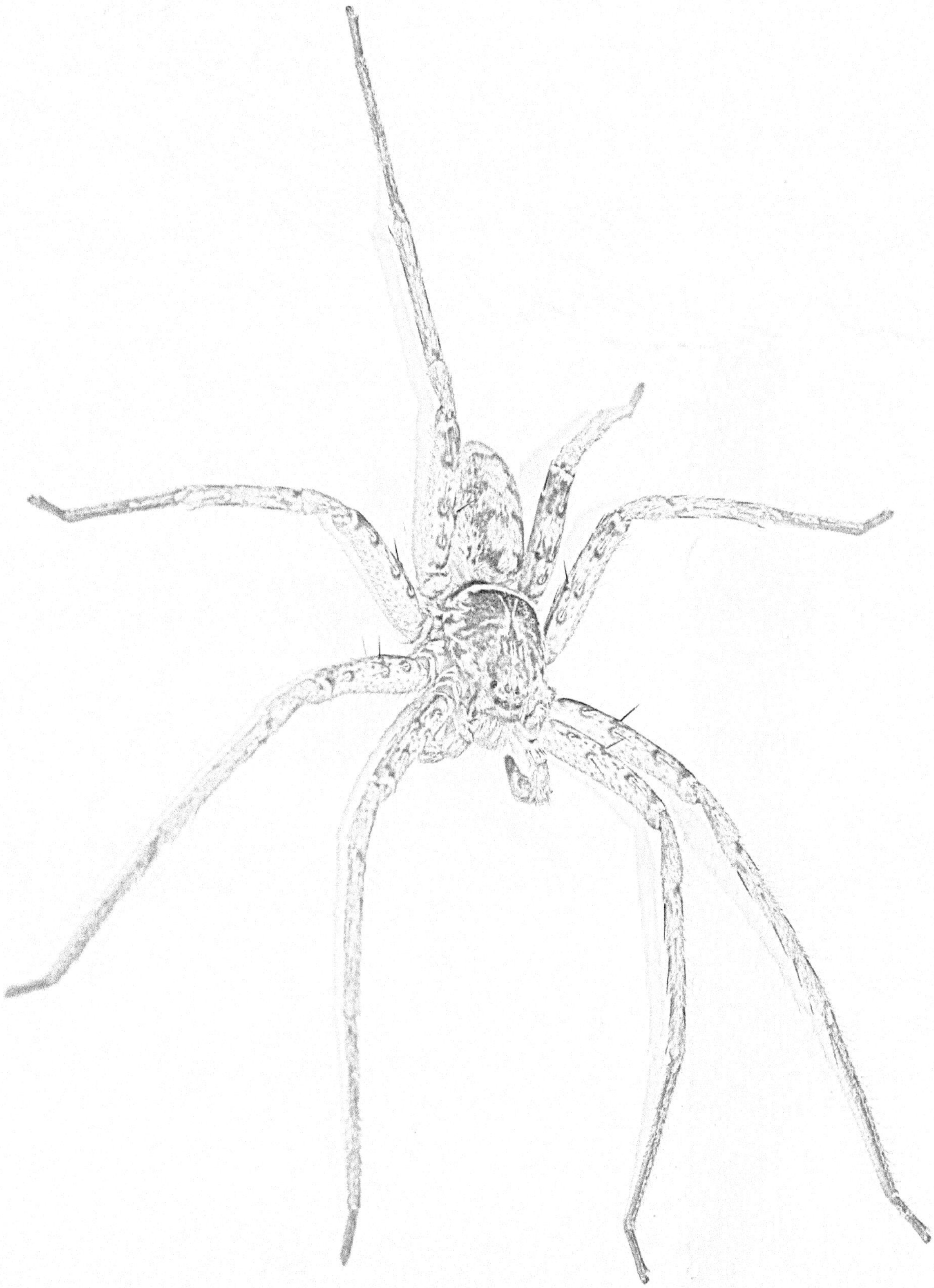

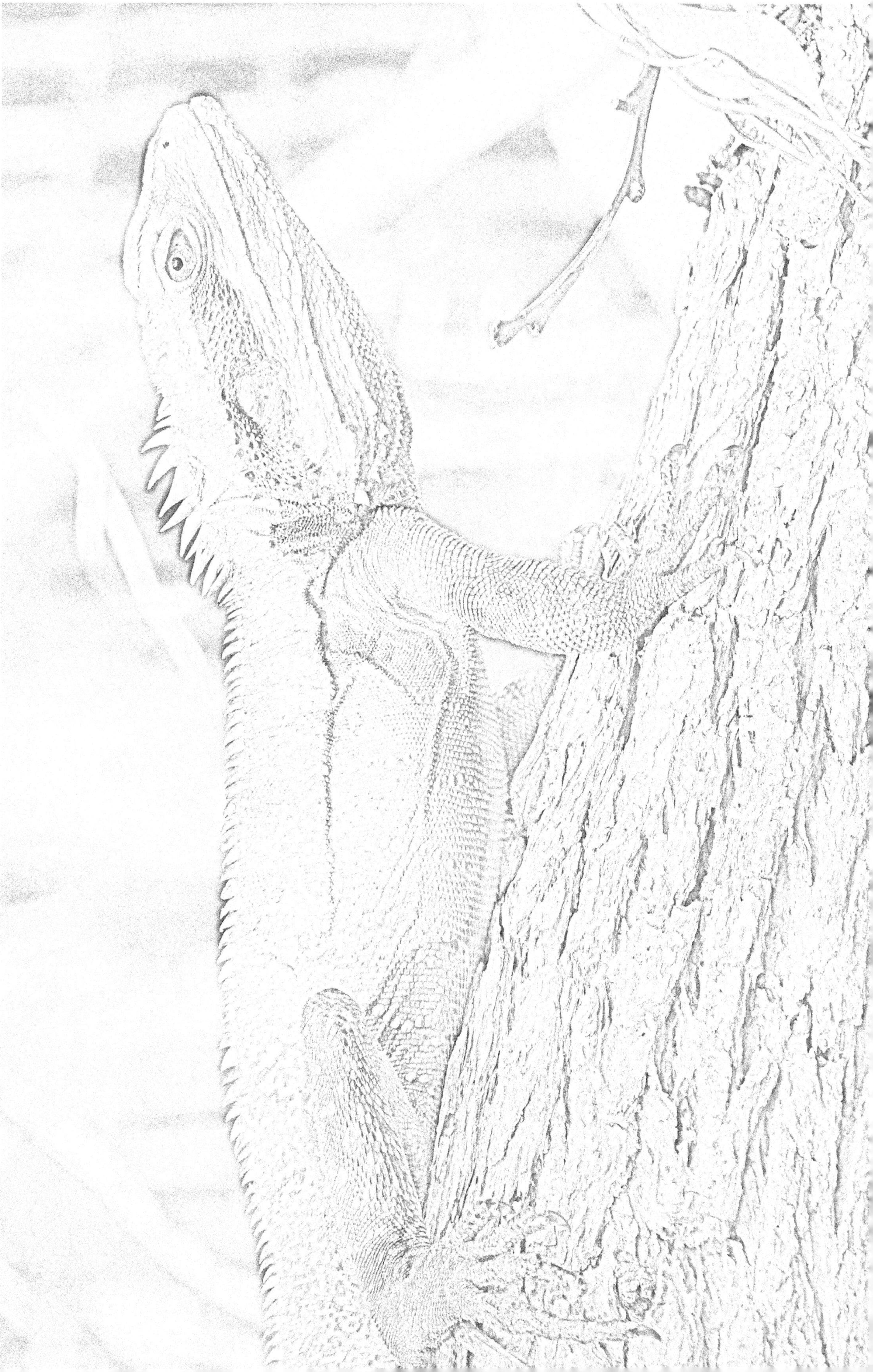

ACT147N
EDGETRACKER
Stessl
MERCURY

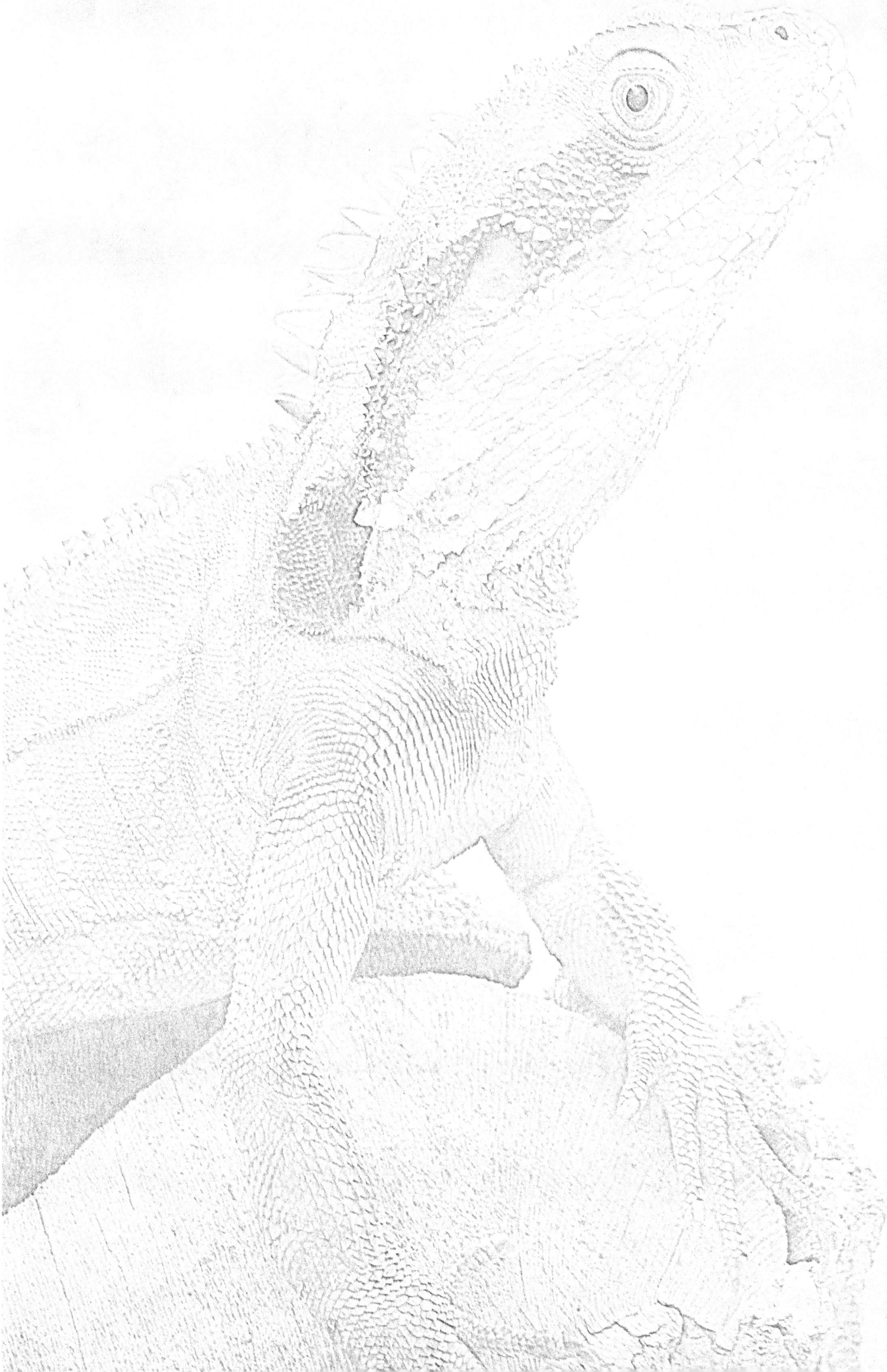

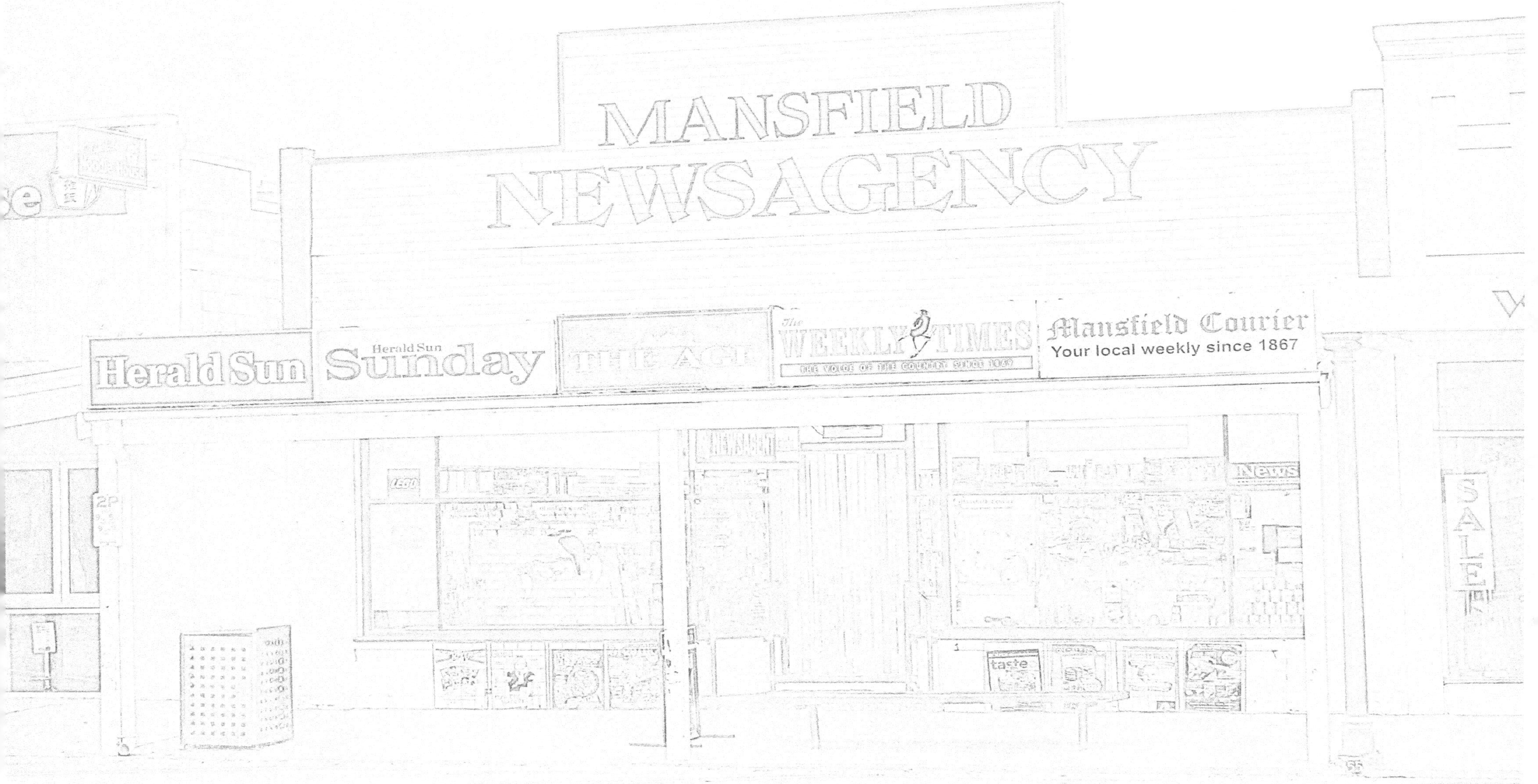
MANSFIELD
NEWSAGENCY
Herald Sun
Herald Sun
Sunday
THE AGE
The
WEEKLY TIMES
THE VOICE OF THE COUNTRY SINCE 1869
Mansfield Courier
Your local weekly since 1867
News
taste
SALE
2P

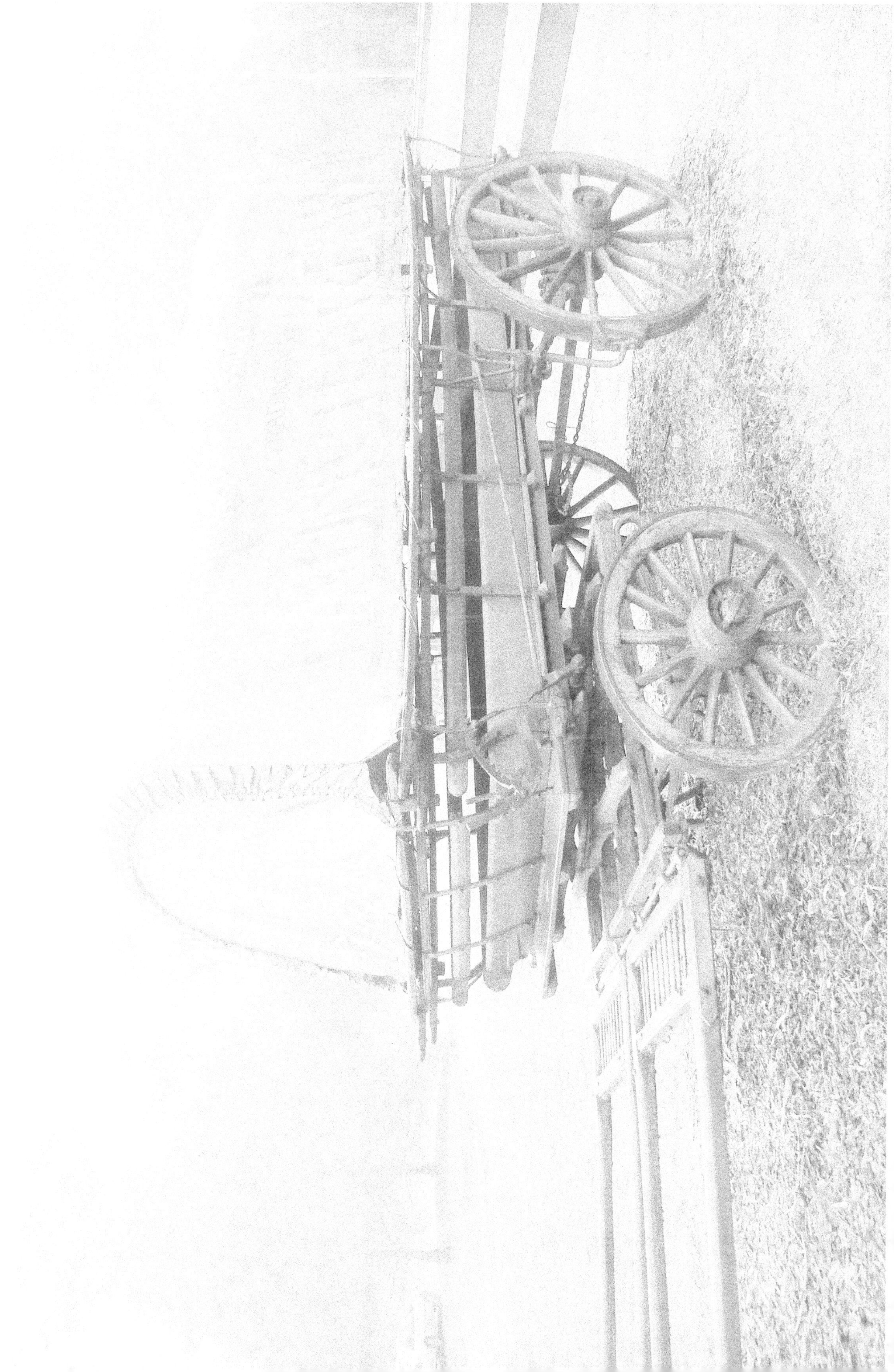

www.ingramcontent.com/pod-product-compliance
Lightning Source LLC
Chambersburg PA
CBHW081050180526
45170CB00005B/1752
* 9 7 8 0 3 5 9 8 2 3 1 4 7 *